Introduction to Data Management Functions and Tools

IDMA 201 COURSE STUDY GUIDE

Insurance Data Management Association (IDMA)
Associate Insurance Data Manager (AIDM)
Designation Program

Technics Publications
BASKING RIDGE, NEW JERSEY

Published by:

2 Lindsey Road
Basking Ridge, NJ 07920 USA

https://www.TechnicsPub.com

Cover design by Lorena Molinari

Edited by the Insurance Data Management Association (IDMA)

First Edition

First Printing 2017

ISBN, print ed.	9781634622493
ISBN, Kindle ed.	9781634622509
ISBN, PDF ed.	9781634622516
ISBN, Enterprise ed.	9781634622523

Library of Congress Control Number: 2017909022

Contents

Introduction

Founded in 1983, IDMA is an independent nonprofit professional association dedicated to increasing the level of professionalism, knowledge, and visibility of insurance data management through education, research, annual forums, local chapter meetings, news bulletins, and peer-to-peer networking. It serves individuals employed in any aspect of insurance data management. This includes individuals engaged in any of the following enterprise information governance activities within various functional areas of insurance companies, regulatory bodies, statistical/rating organizations, industry consulting firms, professional associations and learned societies, and technology research and services providers:

- data definition
- data collection
- data administration
- data standards
- data processing
- data analysis
- internal and external data reporting
- data quality

The main objective of IDMA is the administration of an educational program designed to increase professional proficiency and to provide a professional designation in the data management discipline. Additionally, IDMA provides an ongoing forum for the discussion of issues and innovations in data management through technical seminars, educational workshops, and publications.

IDMA courses, workshops, and forums are highly recommended for a broad audience including new hires, IT and data modeling professionals who want to broaden their knowledge of the business side of insurance data management, anyone who manages and governs data in the industry (statistical, or management information data), and anyone who needs to use or communicate good quality data/information – from actuaries to underwriters, and claims and analytics professionals.

Students who complete the four IDMA-developed courses and successfully pass the examinations are awarded an *Associate Insurance Data Manager (AIDM®)* designation. The IDMA courses may be taken in any order; there are no prerequisites. However, the courses are numbered to indicate a recommended sequence.

Students who complete additional course work from other selected insurance industry educational organizations and successfully pass the specified examinations receive the *Certified Insurance Data Manager (CIDM®)* designation.

For details on the designation requirements, please refer to the IDMA website at www.IDMA.org or call our office at +1 (201) 469-3069.

Using this Course Guide

This course guide will help you learn the course content and prepare for the exam.

Almost all assignments in this course guide, except for the final assignment which is a recap of the prior assignments, include the following components:

- **Educational Objectives**. These are the most important study tools in the course guide. Because all of the questions on the exam are based on the Educational Objectives, the best way to study for the exam is to focus on these objectives.
- **Key Terms and Concepts**. These terms and concepts are fundamental to understanding the assignment. After completing the required reading, test your understanding of the assignment's Key Terms and Concepts by writing their definitions.
- **Review Questions**. The review questions test your understanding of what you have read. Review the Educational Objectives and required reading, then answer the questions to the best of your ability. When you are finished, check the answers at the end of the assignment to evaluate your comprehension.
- **Discussion Questions**. These questions are intended to continue to test your knowledge of the required reading by applying what you've studied to real-life situations. No suggested answers are provided at the end of the assignment for these types of open discussion questions. Answers may vary by student and will depend on their organization's culture, resources, and processes!

Important Note Applicable to All IDMA Course Material: IDMA strives to keep all of its course material current. The information provided is up to date at the time of publication. The timing and pace of industry changes and the constraints of publication can at times result in a lag in updates being included. IDMA regularly reviews content to ensure that it is current and will publish updates as necessary and appropriate.

Exam Information

IDMA exams are given online, consist of one hundred (100) multiple-choice and true/false type questions, and are three hours long. Unofficial scores are tabulated and issued immediately after the exam completion. Official scores are mailed to students within 15 business days after the conclusion of the exam cycle. Passing score is 70%.

Students are allowed to take more than one course exam during an exam cycle. Students are also allowed to retake an exam within the same exam cycle if they were not successful on their first try.

Exams are conducted with no reference materials, papers, books, or other aids permitted in the room. No student may communicate with another during the exam. Students are not allowed to maintain copies of their exam. All exam materials are considered the property of IDMA.

Exam Registration Information and Requirements

Currently, IDMA does not contract with testing centers (such as Prometric, Pearson, Kryterion, etc...) to host its exams onsite. IDMA exams are given, so far as possible, at the student's worksite with cooperation of the human resources or education department in locating a proctor and site.

NOTE: Students are responsible to locate a proctor and provide IDMA with the proctor's contact information. A proctor could be anyone from your HR department, your boss, or staffer. A week prior to the exam, IDMA will email your proctor a "proctor package" explaining the exam process. You will also receive your exam pass via email around the same time.

Purchase of the study guide for the present IDMA course does not automatically register a candidate for the examination. As you proceed with your studies, be sure to arrange for your exam.

- Visit our website at www.IDMA.org to access and print the exam registration form, which contains information and forms needed to register for your exam.
- Plan to register with IDMA well in advance of your exam. Late fees apply two weeks prior to the start of the exam cycle.
- Coordinate with your proctor the date and start time of your exam.

How to Study for IDMA Exams

Use the assigned study materials (textbook and course guide). Focus your study on the Educational Objectives presented at the beginning of each course guide assignment. Thoroughly read the textbook and any other assigned materials, and then complete the course guide exercises. Choose a study method that best suits your needs; for example, participate in traditional class, or informal study group; or study on your own.

IDMA recommends that you begin your studies for the exam at least two months prior to your scheduled exam date.

Student Resources

For more information on any of the IDMA publications, course examinations, and other services:

- Visit our website at www.IDMA.org
- Call us in and outside of the U.S. at +1 (201) 469-3069
- Email our executive director, Farouk Yassine, at fyassine@idma.org
- Fax us at +1 (201) 748-1690
- Write to us at Insurance Data Management Association (IDMA), 545 Washington Boulevard, 16th Floor, Jersey City, NJ 07310

Data, Information, and Knowledge

Educational Objectives

Upon completion of this assignment, you should be able to:

1. Define data, information, and knowledge. Describe the relationship between them.
2. Explain why data and information are assets, and why this is important to both society and organizations.
3. Describe how managers use information and what they do in the absence of information.
4. Describe the role of information in organizational change.
5. Describe why data quality is so important to today's organization.
6. Explain why high data quality is so difficult to maintain.
7. Describe the data lifecycle.
8. Define data architecture.
9. Describe how data architecture and legacy systems impact an organization's ability to obtain the information needed.
10. Define organizational memory and explain its importance.
11. Describe the components of organizational memory.

For each assignment, define or describe each of the Key Terms and Concepts and answer each of the Review and Discussion Questions.

Key Terms and Concepts

Data

Information

Knowledge

Business model

Strategic planning

Tactical planning

Operational planning

Organizational design

Job design

Organizational change

Data quality

Costs of poor data quality ***(Cost of prevention, Cost of correction, and Cost of failure)***

Data conversion

Data architecture

Data architect

Data archive

Data attributes

Legacy system

Data silo

Knowledge management

Organizational memory

Explicit knowledge

Tacit knowledge

Embedded knowledge

Review Questions

1) Define the difference between data, information, and knowledge then describe their relationship.

2) Why are data and information considered assets, and what benefit do they provide to organizations and society?

3) Why must data and information be converted to knowledge for it to be useful to society and organizations?

4) Describe how managers use information.

5) What happens in the absence adequate data? What are the reasons data may be unavailable?

6) What are the four functions of all managers?

7) What is SWOT? Where is it used?

8) Which management group uses tactical planning?

9) Explain how strategic planning, tactical planning, and operational planning work together.

10) Effective managers have interpersonal skills, motivational skills, and leadership skills. How does information play a role in efficient utilization of skills?

11) What controlling measures ensure managers can meet their goals?

12) Describe the role of information in organization change.

13) Explain why the quality of data is critical and must have certain characteristics.

14) In 1992, George Labovitz and Yu Sang Chang developed the 1-10-100 rule. What is the 1-10-100- Rule?

15) What is "raw data"?

16) The most commonly cited functions of all managers are:

A. Budgeting, Organizing, Staffing, and Controlling.

B. Planning, Staffing, Leading, and Purchasing.

C. Planning, Controlling, Leading, and Organizing.

D. Purchasing, Controlling, Leading, and Organizing.

17) In organizations of any size, there are generally three levels of management: senior executives, middle managers, and first-level (or front-line) managers. Describe how each level uses data for planning and how insufficient or inaccurate data impacts the plan.

18) How do managers make decisions in the absence of information?

19) Name the types of changes that drive organizational change.

20) What must information provide to organizations in order for organizational change to be successful?

21) Describe information's role in organizational change.

22) List the five characteristics of data quality.

23) Name the three costs of poor data quality and identify at which cost George Labovitz' and Yu Sang Chang's 1-10-100 Rule would most likely apply.

24) In addition to the direct measurable costs poor data quality has on an organization, there are also hidden costs. Name a few hidden costs that can be caused by poor data quality.

25) Name the three important aspects of data archiving.

26) Which of the following are true regarding the challenges of maintaining high quality data?

I. Data can be intentionally or unintentionally entered incorrectly.

II. Inconsistencies can occur when data are not clearly defined.

III. Multiple systems that are not well-integrated may cause data to be duplicated across those systems.

IV. Data deteriorates over time.

A. I and II only.

B. I and IV only.

C. III and IV only.

D. I, II, III, and IV.

27) Which two steps are considered the operational portion of the data lifecycle and are where data are used to achieve the organization's goals?

A. Create and Acquire and Maintain and Use.

B. Plan and Specify.

C. Enable and Create and Acquire.

D. Plan and Purge.

28) Why are only specific individuals within an organization authorized to purge data?

29) Models, policies, rules, or standards that govern the collection, storage, and arrangement of data in a database system or organization defines which of the following?

A. Data architecture.

B. Database administration.

C. Data conversion.

D. Business model.

30) Data architecture is integral to which stages of the data lifecycle?

I. Planning.

II. Create and acquire.

III. Specify.

IV. Purge.

A. I only.

B. I and III only.

C. II and III only.

D. I, II, and IV.

31) Explain why data architects must have an understanding of the organization's business needs.

32) Explain how the architecture of a legacy system impacts an organization's ability to obtain information.

33) Why is the concept of organizational memory important?

34) True or false, organizational memory comprises any place in which an organization can store data?

Discussion Questions

NOTE: The below questions are intended to continue to challenge you to test your knowledge of the required reading by applying what you have studied to real-life situations.

No suggested answers are provided at the end of the assignment for these types of open discussion questions. Answers may vary by student and will depend on their organization's culture, resources, and processes!

1) Discuss a real-life example of the 1-10-100 Rule.

2) How does your company handle all the unstructured data?

3) Discuss some of the methods you or your colleagues have used to decide or come to a conclusion when information has been insufficient, inaccurate, poorly presented, outdated, or untimely.

Answers to Assignment 1 Questions

NOTE: These answers are provided to give students a basic understanding of acceptable types of responses. They are often not the only valid answers and are not intended to provide an exhaustive response to the questions.

Key Terms and Concepts

Data: Facts about, or attributes of, entities, those things about which an organization wishes to collect or create data.

Information: Data that has been analyzed, processed, or organized for a particular purpose and presented in a relevant and meaningful form and context.

Knowledge: The ability, based on experience and understanding, to use information in a competent, productive way.

Business model: A simple statement of how an organization will generate income.

Strategic planning: A long-term view that articulates the senior management's vision for the organization.

Tactical planning: Involves identifying, selecting and scheduling the activities an organization must complete in order to achieve its strategic objectives.

Operational planning: Facilitates completion of the activities identified in tactical planning.

Organizational design: The structure that best supports the strategic goals of an organization, e.g. centralized or decentralized.

Job design: The management determination of individual job functions to achieve the organization's goals.

Organizational change: The process of using an organization's resources, people, technology, and financial assets to reach a desired future outcome.

Data quality: Data should be accurate, complete, timely and fit for its intended use in operations, decision-making, and planning.

Costs of poor data quality ***(Cost of prevention, Cost of correction, and Cost of failure)*****:**

- **Cost of prevention:** cost of ensuring data is input correctly at the point of data collection.
- **Cost of correction:** cost of verifying and correcting through various operational design stages.
- **Cost of failure:** cost incurred in collecting data incorrectly such that the data fails to perform the desired function.

Data conversion: The process of converting data from one format or structure to another.

Data architecture: The collection of models, policies, rules, or standards that govern which data is collected, and how it is stored, arranged, and put to use in a database system, and/or in an organization.

Data architect: The person responsible for the design, structure, organization, and maintenance of data for a particular company or project.

Data archive: A copy of a database or documents preserved in a secondary, lower cost storage location, for infrequent historical reference and/or recovery; Verb: To move stored data (structured or unstructured) to a secondary, less readily accessed location, at lower storage costs, for historical reference and/or recovery.

Data attributes: A characteristic or fact describing the occurrence of an entity.

Legacy system: Architecture implemented outside of an organization's application architecture. Usually an older application, which may be slated for eventual replacement. Legacy systems are often frustrating because they are difficult to change, few people know exactly what they do, and how they do it, and/or the technology on which they are dependent is becoming obsolete and unsupportable.

Data silo: A repository of fixed data that causes constrain within an organization such that a data system is incompatible or not integrated with other systems. So-called silo data cannot exchange content with other systems in the organization.

Knowledge management: The systematic management of an organization's knowledge assets for the purpose of creating value and meeting tactical and strategic requirements; it consists of the initiatives, processes, strategies, and systems that sustain and enhance the storage, assessment, sharing, refinement, and creation of knowledge.

Organizational memory: The collection of distributed mechanisms for applying past knowledge to current action, residing in humans, culture, information, and communication technologies.

Explicit knowledge: Knowledge that has been codified or documented in some way.

Tacit knowledge: Undocumented knowledge that individuals develop through personal experience.

Embedded knowledge: Knowledge that may have been forgotten but that remains as an artifact within processes, routines, or cultures.

Review Questions

1) Data are facts about or attributes of, entities, those things about which an organization wishes to collect or create data. Date can be expressed as numbers, characters, symbols, or images. Information is data analyzed, processed or organized for a particular purpose and presented in a form and context that are relevant and meaningful. Knowledge is the ability, based on experience and understanding, to use information in a competent, productive way.

2) Data and information are generally recognized as among the most valuable of an organization's assets because of the benefits they provide. Data and information can be considered assets because they can be used to produce value. Managers at all levels use information to plan strategically, tactically and operationally; to organize; to lead; and to control.

3) Data must be interpreted and converted into meaningful and useful information in order to be used productively. Data can provide a competitive advantage by bringing higher quality products to market faster and at lower cost than competitors thus providing better service, reduced costs, and adding value to stakeholders.

4) Executives are responsible for directing the organization as a whole. Middle managers are responsible for achieving the goals established by senior executives. First level or front-line managers help ensure that middle management's plans are successfully implemented to achieve the executives' goals.

5) In the absence of adequate information and market research, an organization's business model, or changes to it, may be flawed. Decisions made without sufficient, accurate information can damage an organization's bottom line. Insufficient, inaccurate, poorly presented, outdated, or untimely information forces decision makers to rely solely on experience, perceptions, and insights which may or may not be correct. When there is an issue or problem to resolve they may ask questions or look for precedents. Often they settle on the first reasonable solution they discover rather than searching for the optimal one. In fact, in the absence of high quality information, a manager's decision is often simply a "best guess". Fortunately, technology and the increasing availability of business information tools allow managers and executives to make better-informed and justified decisions.

6) Planning, Organizing, Leading, and Controlling. In all of these, information is essential.

7) A project or business' Strengths, Weaknesses, Opportunities, and Threats, referred to as "SWOT analysis" is a strategic planning method. SWOT analysis involves recognizing and evaluating an organization's internal strengths and weaknesses relative to its competitors; and identifying external opportunities on which it might capitalize and external threats against which it should guard.

8) Middle managers engage in tactical planning.

9) Just as tactical planning supports the goals established in strategic planning, operational planning facilitates completion of the activities identified in tactical planning. Information supports decision-making at all three levels within an organization.

10) Managers need sufficient information to clearly understand the organization's strategic vision, its objectives, processes, and the environment in which it operates. They also need detailed, accurate, and timely information about the actual performance of both the organization and its employees. Information and performance monitoring allow managers to identify strengths, weaknesses, opportunities, and threats, and to respond appropriately.

11) Managers complete the following tasks: Establish performance benchmarks, compare actual performance to those benchmarks, and take action to correct shortfalls in performance.

12) Organizations need information to: Identify gaps between desired and actual performance; Establish goals that are challenging but realistic; and determine how best to close any identified gaps between actual and desired performance.

13) The Insurance Data Management Association (IDMA) defines data quality as "The degree to which data are fit for their intended uses; data are of high quality if they are fit for their intended uses in operations, decision making, and planning." Data must be: Accurate, Complete, Timely, Relevant, Accessible, and Consistent with an organization's business rules.

14) In manufacturing, quality professionals use the 1-10-100 rule to describe the increasing cost of correcting errors as a product moves from initial design through manufacturing and on to the customer. A problem identified and corrected in the design phase costs relatively little, whereas one identified and corrected during production may cost ten times as much, and one identified after the product has reached the marketplace costs far more.

15) Data without analysis or context, and are meaningless.

16) The correct answer choice is "C".

17) Senior executives use aggregate internal information combined with external data to establish and guide the organization's strategic focus. Mid-level managers use information to perform cost-benefit analyses and evaluate which potential projects would best help achieve the organization's strategic goals. Front-line managers use workflow statistics to improve resource allocation. In the absence of adequate information

and market research, an organization's business model, or changes to it, may be flawed. Decisions made without sufficient, accurate information can damage an organization's bottom line.

18) Decision makers may rely solely on experience, perceptions, and insights which may or may not be correct. When there is an issue or problem to resolve they may ask questions or look for precedents. Often they settle on the first reasonable solution they discover rather than searching for the optimal one. In the absence of high quality information, a manager's decision is often simply a "best guess".

19) The types of changes that drive organizational change are: Competitors' products and services; Laws and regulations; Customer needs, tastes, and expectations; Methods of doing business; and Technology.

20) Organizations need information to identify gaps between desired and actual performance, establish goals that are challenging but realistic; and determine how best to close any identified gaps between actual and desired performance.

21) Information provides a catalyst for organizational change. As an organization acquires more data and uses them more effectively it becomes more agile. It is better able to understand its environment and to adjust its focus, structure, processes, and relationships to respond to environmental changes.

22) Accurate; Complete; Timely; Consistent; and Relevant.

23) Cost of prevention – 1; Cost of correction – 10; and Cost of failure – 100.

24) Hidden costs of poor data quality that an organization can suffer are: The value of lost opportunities; Loss of knowledge through employee turnover; Business losses resulting from inappropriate strategic decisions; Long lead times; Data being registered multiple times; Focus on wrong customer segments; Poor overall production planning; and poor price policies.

25) Data must be stored in a format that will make them readily accessible when required; the form in which archived data are stored must be kept current; and sufficient data should be retained to ensure subsequent analysis yields meaningful information.

26) The correct answer choice is "D".

27) The correct answer choice is "A".

28) Because purged data cannot be retrieved, and because errors in purging can cause damage to a system.

29) The correct answer choice is "A".

30) The correct answer choice is "B".

31) Data architecture identifies data created and used by multiple functional units to ensure that data interactions are documented and accounted for during system design. Without an understanding of the organization's business needs, developers could create separate application systems for each of the functional units.

32) They were typically designed to collect, store, and manipulate data for a single purpose and were not designed to integrate with other systems. This lack of integration results in business information silos. Silos constrain information within a system, a department, or a functional unit, and do not allow it to be shared across the organization.

33) The concept of organizational memory is important because it implies an organization's ability to acquire, retain, retrieve, and apply knowledge from previously unrecognized sources to make more effective decisions about current issues.

34) False. Organizational memory comprises any place in which an organization can store knowledge.

Introduction to Data Management

Educational Objectives

Upon completion of this assignment, you should be able to:

1. Define data management.
2. Describe the goals of data management.
3. Provide the business case for data management.
4. Describe the data management functions key to meeting the goals.
5. Describe the roles of individuals in data management.
6. Describe the roles of various organizational units in data management.
7. Explain why successful data management requires an understanding of both organizational behavior and information technology.
8. Define enterprise data management.
9. Describe the core functions and key roles in enterprise data management.
10. Describe the challenges to implementing enterprise data management.
11. Describe the purpose of the data manager.
12. List the key data manager functions.
13. Describe where in an organization data managers can be located.
14. Describe the interactions between data managers and business analysts, front line managers, executives, and IT professionals.
15. Describe the critical skills of successful data managers.
16. Describe the data manager's role at different phases of the Data Lifecycle.
17. Describe the role of professionalism in data management and explain why it is integral to success.
18. List and describe data management best practices.

For each assignment, define or describe each of the Key Terms and Concepts and answer each of the Review and Discussion Questions.

Key Terms and Concepts

Data security

Data integrity

Data integration

Data warehouse

Data federation

Data governance

Data architecture management

Enterprise data model

Data development

Data model

Data operations management

Database support

Data technology management

Data security management

Master data

Reference data

Data marts

Business intelligence (BI)

Document management

Content management

Metadata management

Data quality management

Data modelers/consultants

Business intelligence analysts

Data/reporting analysts

Database administrators

Data security administrators

Collaborators

Data brokers

Data stewardship

Business data owners

Business data stewards

Data stewardship team or data stewardship steering committee

Technical data stewards

Executive data stewards

Data management services

Data governance council (DGC)

Data governance office (DGO)

Organizational behavior

Organizational behavioral frameworks. Frameworks within which organizations can operate, such as:

Autocratic framework:

Custodial framework:

Supportive framework:

Collegial organization:

System framework:

Enterprise data management or enterprise information management (EIM)

Business process model

Review Questions

1) Define data management.

2) List the goals the business function of data management focuses on achieving.

3) What does it mean to use data effectively?

4) Which data management function involves managing the day-to-day operation of the organization's systems and focuses on database performance, and data integrity and availability?

   A. Metadata management.

   B. Master data management.

   C. Content management.

   D. Data operations management.

5) What is the goal of master and reference data management?

6) List the goals of metadata management.

7) Briefly describe the four stages of data quality management (DQM).

8) A successful data management program requires the sponsorship and support of a data management executive. What is the data management executive sponsor responsible for?

9) Where data management functions reside, and how they will be performed, and to whom the responsibility is assigned, depend to a great extent on what?

10) Describe the formal groups commonly involved in an organization's data management and data stewardship activities including the make-up of each group's participants and their role.

11) Which one of the following statements is NOT true?

A. Business data owners work with data stewards to ensure that essential data are identified, defined, used, and managed so as to support operational functions.

B. Business data stewards identify and define data and metadata requirements; draft data model specifications; define business rules and data quality requirements; identify and help resolve data issues; and assist in evaluating and improving the quality of the organization's data.

C. Executive data stewards exercise stewardship at the most senior level. This is a role held by a senior manager sitting on the data governance council, accountable for the data quality and data practices within a department, for planning and oversight of data management programs, and appointment of other data stewards.

D. None of the above.

12) Why is it important that data management professionals understand organizational behavior?

13) Which of the following best describe enterprise data management?

V. Can help eliminate information silos.

VI. Can lead to increased integration and alignment among the functional areas.

VII. Can result in enhanced strategic and tactical decision making.

VIII. Can be inflexible and unable to meet the needs of a rapidly changing environment.

A. I and IV.

B. II only.

C. I, II, and III.

D. III only.

14) Describe the role of an enterprise information management (EIM) champion.

15) Which data management activities play a key role in implementing an EIM?

16) List the components of a successful EIM system.

17) Describe the challenges to implementing an EIM.

18) What is the role of the data manager?

19) Which one of the following statements is NOT true?

A. Data managers help analyze an organization's data and information needs, and assist in the development, implementation, and maintenance of the technical solutions required to meet those needs.

B. Data managers engage in a variety of activities requiring technical skills such as business process modeling.

C. Data managers usually do not participate in the development of the enterprise data strategy and enterprise data model that supports the strategy.

D. Data managers conduct data analysis and work with data stewards and others to enhance and maintain data quality.

20) Describe where in an organization data managers can be located.

21) Describing the skills that are critical for a successful data manager, which one of the following statements is NOT true?

A. Understands the business environment in which the organization operates as well as its strategic and tactical focus.

B. Keeps current with new technologies and techniques for managing data effectively.

C. Always able to convince others of the value of data management initiatives and to secure their commitment and participation.

D. None of the above.

22) Which statement best describes how data managers use both their technical and interpersonal skills at each stage in the data lifecycle?

A. To enhance data quality, security, integrity, integration, and access to information.

B. To ensure that the organization's requirements for quality data are met; and review data quality audits.

C. To ensure that data warehouses and data marts are appropriately integrated and not redundant.

D. All of the above.

23) Supporting data management and data quality on an individual as well as an organizational level best describes which data management best practice?

A. Data and Data Quality Standards.

B. Privacy Issues.

C. Individual Support.

D. Operations and Processes.

24) What is the “best practice” for Data Element Development and Specification?

25) What is the business case for data management?

26) The process of analyzing an organization’s strategies, structures, and processes to identify all of the data it requires and then developing a theoretical framework within which to meet those requirements best describes which of the following:

A. Data governance.

B. Data architecture management.

C. Data security management.

D. Data steward.

27) Which of the following is NOT considered a function of data development?

A. Testing of the system.

B. Documentation and training.

C. Monitoring the effectiveness of policies and procedures.

D. Installation and deployment.

28) List the seven steps of the system development lifecycle.

29) Explain the difference between master data and reference data and give examples of each.

30) Describe data warehouse and the steps in data warehousing.

31) How can an organization implement enterprise information management (EIM)?

32) True or false, the data stewardship team is a temporary or permanent focused group of business data stewards collaborating on data modeling, specification and data quality improvement, typically in an assigned subject area, led by a coordinating data steward and facilitated by a data architect?

33) Which one of the following statements is NOT true?

A. Data architects develop and maintain the enterprise data model and ensure that data warehouses and data marts are appropriately integrated and not redundant.

B. Business intelligence analysts design and maintain the business intelligence user environment and train users in its application.

C. Data security administrators select or design the appropriate software, implement the software, and control its use to ensure a proper structure for the data.

D. Data/reporting analysts document, interpret, and maintain controls on the data, and develop or assist in the development of external and internal reports.

Discussion Questions

NOTE: The below questions are intended to continue to challenge you to test your knowledge of the required reading by applying what you have studied to real-life situations.

No suggested answers are provided at the end of the assignment for these types of open discussion questions. Answers may vary by student and will depend on their organization's culture, resources, and processes!

1) Data management focuses on enhancing data quality, ensuring data security, maintaining data integrity, increasing data integration, and improving access to information. Discuss which area or areas of focus your responsibility falls under and explain how this is accomplished.

2) Think about the data managers you interact with on a daily basis in your organization and discuss where in the organization they are located.

3) Once again, thinking about the data managers you interact with on a daily basis in your organization; discuss the technical skills that are required for their success. What interpersonal skills do the data managers possess?

4) The textbook lists 10 key data management activities. Name the activities that you recognize in your organization. Are some combined? Does a group or an individual perform the activities? Which activities do you execute, if any?

5) IDMA's Standards for Professionalism for Insurance Data Managers defines the high level of professional conduct and ethical standards data managers demanded by the data manager's responsibility. Explain the commitment and guideline that most resonates with you and why.

Answers to Assignment 2 Questions

NOTE: These answers are provided to give students a basic understanding of acceptable types of responses. They are often not the only valid answers and are not intended to provide an exhaustive response to the questions.

Key Terms and Concepts

Data security: The degree to which data is kept confidential and protected from unauthorized access, use, or alteration.

Data integrity: The accuracy, uniformity, and reliability of the values used to store and manipulate data. It is concerned with how well the data conforms to established standards, formats, and business rules.

Data integration: The process of combining data from a variety of sources to create useful information. It is the planned and controlled transformation and flow of data across databases, for operational and/or analytical use.

Data warehouse: An integrated, centralized decision support database and the related software programs used to collect, cleanse, transform, and store data from a variety of operational sources.

Data federation: The aggregators of data from different sources in a virtual database.

Data governance: The exercise of authority, control, and shared decision-making (planning, monitoring and enforcement) over the management of data assets.

Data architecture management: The process of analyzing an organization's strategies, structures, and processes to identify all of the data it requires and then developing a theoretical framework within which to meet those requirements.

Enterprise data model: A common consistent view and understanding of data elements and their relationships across the enterprise.

Data development: The lifecycle of panning, analyzing, designing, building, testing, deploying, and maintaining the data.

Data model: A graphical representation of data to help determine data requirements, design, and the relationships among them.

Data operations management: A planning, control, and support for structured data assets across the data lifecycle, from creation and acquisition through archival and purge.

Database support: Includes activities such as monitoring and tuning the performance of the organization's databases; planning and implementing procedures for data backup and recovery; data archiving, retention, and purging; and supporting specialized databases.

Data technology management: Involves evaluating, selecting, and implementing hardware and software solutions to meet the organization's needs.

Data security management: Management functions of developing, implementing, and monitoring the effectiveness of policies and procedures that ensure confidentiality of data and information for the organizations' own good as well as to meet with compliance requirements.

Master data: Data about things that are important to the organization used for integration for use by a variety of systems.

Reference data: Data used to categorize other data and can include such things as codes and flags. Standardized reference data support integration and the sharing of information.

Data marts: Subsets of the data warehouse that focus on a particular subject area enabling quicker response times and facilitating use by limiting data selection options.

Business intelligence (BI): The ability to query an organization's stores of data to allow managers to gain a greater insight for strategic, tactical, and operational planning.

Document management: A collection of systems used to maintain, classify, organize, and retrieve electronic documents.

Content management: The organizing, categorizing, and structuring of information resources so that they can be stored, published, and reused in multiple ways.

Metadata management: Planning, implementation, and control activities to enable easy access to high quality, integrated metadata.

Data quality management: An iterative process of planning, deploying, monitoring, and acting to ensure data meets the standards of established benchmarks.

Data modelers/consultants: Determine data requirements, integrate the various data components into data models, identify the means of capturing the data, develop or approve the business rules associated with the data, and define data quality requirements.

Business intelligence analysts: Design and maintain the business intelligence user environment and train users in its application.

Data/reporting analysts: Professionals that document, interpret, and maintain controls on the data, and develop or assist in the development of external and internal reports.

Database administrators: Select or design the appropriate software, implement the software, and control its use to ensure a proper structure for the data.

Data security administrators: Professionals that ensure controlled access to classified data.

Collaborators: Groups with whom organizations develop data sharing agreements.

Data brokers: People who supply data processing and metadata support by subscription.

Data stewardship: The formal, specifically assigned, and entrusted accountability for business (non-technical) responsibilities ensuring effective control and use of data and information assets.

Business data owners: Individuals involved in an organization's various operational areas and are often responsible for the primary creators, acquirers, and users of data.

Business data stewards: Subject matter experts (SMEs) who are responsible for a particular segment of the organization or a specific subject area. A business data steward's role is to identify and define data and metadata requirements; draft data model specifications; define business rules and data quality requirements; identify and help resolve data issues; and assist in evaluating and improving the quality of the organization's data.

Data stewardship team or data stewardship steering committee: A focused group of business data stewards collaborating on data modeling, specification, and data quality improvement, typically in an assigned subject area, led by a coordinating data steward and facilitated by a data architect.

Technical data stewards: Members of the IT department who focus on the organization's technical data requirements.

Executive data stewards: Professionals that exercise data stewardship at the most senior level.

Data management services: A unit or group of units responsible for data management.

Data governance council (DGC): A cross-functional group with members from both IT and the organization's operations.

Data governance office (DGO): Office of coordinators involved in activities such as scheduling of data governance and stewardship meetings; preparing agendas and minutes; ensuring that data modeling and data architecture activities include representatives from the operational side of the organization; and assisting in other data stewardship initiatives.

Organizational behavior: The elements of psychology, anthropology, sociology, and economics in an organization's structure and culture, the leadership style, the characteristics of the teams within the organization, and the ways in which the organization communicates internally and externally.

Organizational behavioral frameworks. Frameworks within which organizations can operate, such as:

- **Autocratic** framework: the traditional business model in which managers' focus is on authority,
- **Custodial** framework: management's orientation is financial,
- **Supportive** framework: managers are concerned with leadership and supporting employees to encourage and enhance performance,
- **Collegial** organization: management focuses on partnership and teamwork, empowering employees to participate more actively, and
- **System** framework: management focuses on building a culture of community in which employees take ownership and are passionately committed to the organization's success.

Enterprise data management or **enterprise information management (EIM):** A model for data management performed with an enterprise-wide mandate.

Business process model: A tool for understanding and graphically describing the processes within an organization.

Review Questions

1) Data management is a discipline focused on enhancing the value of data and information. It is the process of planning, defining, organizing, maintaining, and managing access to digitally created, stored, and transmitted data that are of relevance and use to an organization.

2) The goals the business function of data management focuses on achieving are: Understanding the data; Enhancing data quality; Ensuring data security; Maintaining data integrity; Increasing data integration; and Improving access to information.

3) It is important to understand what data signify. Each piece of data needs to be clearly defined in terms of what it means, how it is represented, how it is acquired or created, and how it is to be used.

4) The correct answer choice is "D".

5) The goal of master and reference data management is to ensure consistency with a 'golden version' of data values.

6) Metadata management: Ensures that metadata terminology and practices are consistent and clearly understood across the organization; Integrates metadata from various sources within the organization; Facilitates access to metadata; and Ensures the quality and security of the organization's metadata.

7) The four stages of data quality management (DQM) are:

- Planning – develops a plan to assess the organization's data, identify the target level of data quality required to meet business needs, establish standards or benchmarks for measuring data quality, and create business rules to support high quality data.
- Deploy – compares actual data quality with the standards established in the planning phase, identifies the sources of data quality problems, and implements solutions.
- Monitor – ensures that the corrective measures implemented have been successful.
- Act – if data quality remains unchanged or deteriorates, the DQM team will work to identify the cause or causes and take corrective action.

8) Overseeing data governance and data stewardship; developing data management staff, and interceding where necessary in data management projects.

9) Size, structure, focus, and culture.

10) The formal groups are:

A. Data management services – a unit or group of units responsible for data management and include a variety of data management professionals, such as data architects, analysts, security specialists, metadata specialists and decision-support specialists.

B. Data governance council (DGC) – a cross-functional group which generally includes the chief information officer (CIO), the data management (DM) leader, and a business executive who acts as chief data steward. It is not uncommon for this group to include executives representing other functions, such as actuarial, underwriting, and claims. The DGC makes high level, strategic decisions about data governance as an integrated function within the organization.

C. Data stewardship steering committee – a group comprising members from both IT and multiple operational or business functions. It is responsible for overseeing data management initiatives identified by the DGC. The steering committee is made up of coordinating data stewards.

D. Data governance office (DGO) – act as coordinators, scheduling data governance and stewardship meetings; preparing agendas and minutes; ensuring that data modeling and data architecture activities include representatives from the operational side of the organization; and assisting in other data stewardship initiatives.

11) The correct answer choice is "D".

12) Organizational behavior can have a significant impact on the success of data management initiatives. Individuals and organizations are often resistant to change, new technologies, and the changes in business processes and operational roles associated with them, can be daunting for non-technical members of the organization. Technological changes implemented to help achieve strategic objectives will generally earn a greater return on investment if all of the organization's employees embrace those changes. Effective data management requires commitment and participation through all levels and across all functional areas within the organization. Data management professionals who understand organizational behavior are better able to create a culture that promotes commitment, cooperation, and participation in data management activities at all levels.

13) The correct answer choice is "C".

14) Usually at a senior level within the organization. This individual's role would be to ensure that an EIM focus is integrated into all data management activities and that senior executives understand the relevance of EIM and the competitive advantage it can deliver.

15) Data governance, data stewardship, metadata management, and data architecture management.

16) Careful planning, strong leadership, considerable investment, and significant technical expertise.

17) EIM may require the organization to restructure itself, its business processes, and its internal and external relationships. Often, an enterprise's approach to data management is fragmented because the organization itself is fragmented. It is not enough to focus on data, systems, and technology when implementing an EIM initiative; a successful EIM implementation requires consideration of the enterprise as a whole. EIM professionals need to develop the soft skills necessary to recognize and manage the organizational behavior and cultural issues that are critical success factors in any significant organizational change.

18) To provide business managers with the information they need to accomplish the objectives of the organization.

19) The correct answer choice is "C".

20) Depending on the size, structure and culture of an enterprise, data managers may be located in a variety of areas. Some organizations centralize the data management function, others distribute data management responsibilities across multiple units, still others embed at least some data management responsibilities in operational units in the form of data stewards.

21) The correct answer choice is "D".

22) The correct answer choice is "A".

23) The correct answer choice is "D".

24) Design and maintain data, systems, and reporting mechanisms in a manner that promotes good data management and data quality.

25) The data management function improves access to information. Decision makers have better information faster, which increases the likelihood that the organization will succeed strategically, tactically,

operationally, and competitively. Effective data management can also result in operational efficiencies. It can allow an organization to respond more quickly to change. It can improve an organization's effectiveness by identifying sales opportunities or enhancing customer satisfaction. It can allow an organization to tailor products and services for individual customers. It can improve an organization's ability to comply with regulatory requirements. Finally, it can help ensure that an organization's information technology (IT) is closely aligned with its business goals and strategies.

26) The correct answer choice is "B".

27) The correct answer choice is "C".

28) Plan, Analyze, Design, Build, Test, Deploy, and Maintain.

29) Master data are data about things that are important to the organization, such as customers, employees, regional offices, products, accounts, or a fleet of trucks. Within an organization these data are typically used by multiple systems. For example, an individual customer's data can exist in an underwriting system, a claims system, and an accounting system.

    Reference data are data used to categorize other data and can include such things as codes and flags. For example, a code may indicate that a claim has been received but not yet assigned to a claims adjuster.

30) Data warehouse is a database used to support decision-making within an organization. The data are transformed from their original format to the format required by the data warehouse and then they are loaded into the database. This is referred to as "extract-transform-load" (ETL) and software programs perform the ETL processes.

31) Successful implementation of an EIM strategy requires careful planning, strong leadership, a considerable investment, and significant technical expertise. It may also require the organization to restructure itself, its business processes, and its internal and external relationships.

32) True.

33) The correct answer choice is "C".

Data Standards

Educational Objectives

Upon completion of this assignment, you should be able to:

1. Define standards.
2. Explain why standards matter and what standards do.
3. Describe the role of standards development organizations (SDOs).
4. Identify the purpose of the major SDO's, including the International Organization for Standardization (ISO), the American National Standards Institute (ANSI), the Association for Cooperative Operations Research and Development (ACORD), the International Association of Industrial Accident Boards and Commissions (IAIABC), and the Workers Compensation Insurance Organizations (WCIO).
5. Identify organizations other than SDOs that impact or define standards.
6. Discuss the rationale for data sharing.
7. Define electronic data interchange (EDI).
8. Define the structure and rules for standard data element names.
9. Name the "representation" or "class words" for data elements.

For each assignment, define or describe each of the Key Terms and Concepts and answer each of the Review and Discussion Questions.

Key Terms and Concepts

Standard

Standards development organizations (SDOs)

International Organization for Standardization (ISO)

Conformity assessment

American National Standards Institute (ANSI)

Association for Cooperative Operations Research and Development (ACORD)

Value chain

International Association of Industrial Accident Boards and Commissions (IAIABC)

Workers Compensation Insurance Organizations (WCIO)

Underwriting cycle

Data collection organization (DCOs)

Electronic data interchange (EDI)

Data mapping

Data element

Domain

Object

Property term

Representation or class term

Data dictionary

Review Questions

1) Explain the difference between regulatory standards and voluntary standards.

2) Why are standards important?

3) How can standards reduce costs for producers and consumers?

4) Explain the difference between a traditional transaction and an electronic data interchange (EDI) transaction. Give examples of each.

5) Which of the following are true regarding how data standards can facilitate the exchange of insurance information?

I. Increased rating and pricing.

II. Increased profitability.

III. Increased operational efficiency.

IV. Increased business processes.

A. II and III only.

B. II only.

C. I and III only.

D. III and IV only.

6) Which of the following are true regarding the three common parts of data element names?

I. Object.

II. Include verbs.

III. Can only be one word.

IV. Representation or class term.

A. I only.

B. I and IV.

C. III only.

D. I, II and IV.

7) What is the definition of a standard?

8) An organization must have which of the following in order for quality standards to be effective?

A. A system to measure actual performance to the standard.

B. A code of conduct.

C. A common technical vocabulary.

D. Standard, language independent signs.

9) Which of the following statements best describe the role of a Standards Development Organization (SDO)?

I. Develop new standards.

II. Review underwriting and claims settlement procedures.

III. Maintain current standards.

IV. Attempt to coordinate with existing standards.

A. I and II.

B. I, II, and III.

C. I, III, and IV.

D. All of the above.

10) Which SDO works to create standards that reflect international consensus?

A. International Association of Industrial Accident Boards and Commissions (IAIABC).

B. International Organization for Standardization (ISO).

C. Association for Cooperative Operations Research and Development (ACORD).

D. Committee on Consumer Policy (COPALCO).

11) Name the SDOs that focus specifically on the insurance industry and briefly describe their purpose.

12) Other than SDOs, what organizations or groups define, develop, and/or impact standards?

A. Labor unions.

B. Consumer groups.

C. Professional membership groups.

D. All of the above.

13) List the entities with which insurers would share data.

14) List the entities from which insurers would obtain data.

15) Define electronic data interchange (EDI).

16) Describe how EDI reduces errors and inefficiencies.

17) A specific characteristic of a person, thing, process, transaction, or concept, describes which of the following?

    A. Domain.

    B. Data element.

    C. Property term.

    D. Object.

18) List and briefly describe the three common parts of a data element.

19) Explain how Rule 12, in the Standard Data Element Rules, achieves data quality.

20) The statement, "new data elements must not be developed to identify specific classes of risk/coverages, which are uniquely identified by other elements" describes which data element rule?

21) Which of the following is NOT a data element rule?

    A. Variable Field Lengths.

    B. Need for Flexibility.

    C. Conversion and Combination of Data.

    D. Mappability.

22) Which data standard rule, or rules, addresses the maintenance of the data elements, standards, and guidelines?

23) Which of the following are examples of “representation” or “class words”?

A. Employee, address, length.

B. Age, insured, date.

C. Year, state, name.

D. Code, factor, rate.

24) What does data dictionary consist of?

25) Who imposes data standards in the insurance industry and in what areas do they exist?

26) Who develops standards and why?

27) List the steps in the standards development lifecycle.

28) What are the goals for rate regulation?

29) Why might regulators review an insurer's underwriting and claims procedures?

30) What does NAIC stand for and what is its purpose?

31) Explain the role of International Organization for Standardization (ISO) in data standards organizations.

32) What is ANSI's (American National Standards Institute's) mission?

33) What is conformity assessment and how is it achieved?

34) Explain the difference between a ‘soft market’ and a ‘hard market’.

35) Why is insurer solvency so important to regulators?

36) Which of the following are true regarding standard data element rules?

I. Commonality is a goal to work toward, but should not be a constraint.

II. Coding structures must be rigid and inflexible.

III. Field lengths should be variable.

IV. Fields may have multiple definitions.

A. I only.

B. II only.

C. I and III only.

D. III and IV only.

Discussion Questions

NOTE: The below questions are intended to continue to challenge you to test your knowledge of the required reading by applying what you have studied to real-life situations.

No suggested answers are provided at the end of the assignment for these types of open discussion questions. Answers may vary by student and will depend on their organization's culture, resources, and processes!

1) Think about the products you use on a daily basis. Which ones apply standards consistently? Which ones don't? Discuss how those products that don't apply standards consistently can improve.

2) Name some of the entities that you or your organization share data with, and those that you obtain data from. Discuss why you share, or obtain data from these entities.

3) Identify processes in your organization that use EDI and discuss any process that would be improved by EDI.

4) Reviewing Standard Data Element Rules (included in the course textbook); identify the rules that may be difficult to apply and discuss why.

Answers to Assignment 3 Questions

NOTE: These answers are provided to give students a basic understanding of acceptable types of responses. They are often not the only valid answers and are not intended to provide an exhaustive response to the questions.

Key Terms and Concepts

Standard: A document that provides requirements, specifications, guidelines or characteristics that can be used consistently to ensure that materials, products, processes, and services are fit for their purpose.

Standards development organizations (SDOs): Organizations that create standards through collaborative and consultative manner.

International Organization for Standardization (ISO): A non-governmental body with member organizations from over 160 countries who works to create standards that reflect international consensus with input from other countries of the world.

Conformity assessment: The process of determining whether an organization's products or services actually comply with the requirements outlined in a particular ISO standard.

American National Standards Institute (ANSI): A private, nonprofit organization that is a representative of the United States to the ISO.

Association for Cooperative Operations Research and Development (ACORD): A nonprofit organization for the development and implementation of data standards that facilitate the exchange of insurance information.

Value chain: An end-to-end set of activities initiated by a request from a customer (external or internal) and resulting in a benefit delivered to that customer.

International Association of Industrial Accident Boards and Commissions (IAIABC): A nonprofit trade association of member agencies charged with the administration and regulation of workers' compensation; workers' compensation professionals, insurers, medical providers, law firms, and organizations involved in the electronic exchange of workers' compensation data.

Workers Compensation Insurance Organizations (WCIO): A voluntary association of statutorily authorized or licensed rating, advisory, or data service organizations that collect workers compensation insurance information in one or more states. WCIO develops and maintains standards for the electronic transmission of data to and from rating and advisory organizations.

Underwriting cycle: The relaxing or tightening of underwriting standards and correspondingly decrease or increase rates due to market and competitive pressures.

Data collection organizations (DCOs): Organizations authorized to collect and submit data on behalf of insurers to regulators as required by the regulators.

Electronic data interchange (EDI): A standards-driven technology for high volume B2B (business to business) e-business transaction exchange, linking application systems across enterprises, so that a transaction on one system at one company generates a like transaction on a system at another company.

Data mapping: The assignment of source data elements to target data elements.

Data element: An item of information, such as a date of birth or risk classification.

Domain: A set of values, all of the same data type.

Object: The first part of a data element that identifies the entity.

Property term: The second part of a data element that specifies the property, or characteristic, of the entity to which the data element refers.

Representation or **class term:** The third part of a data element used to categorize it into a particular data type.

Data dictionary: A record of data elements that typically includes the data element names, a description of the information provided by each data element, and any associated business and/or technical metadata required by internal and external users of the system.

Review Questions

1) Regulatory standards are drafted and enforced by government agencies. Voluntary standards are developed through collaboration and negotiation.

2) Standards are important because they provide a foundation for success. They facilitate communication, support quality, and consistency in products and services.

3) Standardization places limits on the number of product alternatives made available. For example, while many commercial insurance policies are customized for particular insureds, for any given insurer the majority of personal lines policies are standardized. This standardization simplifies underwriting, policy issuance and claims handling, and facilitates process automation. This in turn reduces operating costs for the insurer and premiums for its insureds.

4) In a traditional transaction for example, a purchaser identifies the items an organization needs, completes an order form and enters it into the company's system. He or she then mails, faxes, or emails the order to the company's supplier. At the supplier's office, employees enter the order information into the company's production, shipping and accounting systems. When the order is fulfilled, an employee at the supplier's office generates an invoice, which is mailed, faxed or emailed to the purchaser. The purchaser enters receipt of the goods in the company's inventory system and the invoice in the accounting system. The process is time-consuming; it involves a number of steps and delays; and each time data are manually entered, the possibility for errors is introduced.

   In an EDI-based transaction, different systems at different organizations, or within the same organization, can "talk" to each other in a common format, eliminating the need for human involvement at multiple stages in the process. This reduces errors and inefficiencies.

5) The correct answer choice is "A".

6) The correct answer choice is "B".

7) A document that provides requirements, specifications, guidelines or characteristics that can be used consistently to ensure that materials, products, processes, and services are fit for their purpose.

8) The correct answer choice is “A”.

9) The correct answer choice is “C”.

10) The correct answer choice is “B”.

11) ACORD–facilitates the development of open consensus data standards and forms and works with its members to drive implementation of those standards.

    IAIABC–serves as an expert resource for research, policies, best practices, and standards; provides a forum to share information, discusses issues and solutions; assists in identifying cost reduction opportunities; develops, analyzes, and promulgates standards.

    WCIO–develops and maintains standards for the electronic transmission of data to rating and advisory organizations.

12) The correct answer choice is “D”.

13) Producers, reinsurers, regulators, advisory organizations, law enforcement, fraud prevention organizations, and industry associations.

14) Government agencies, independent claims services, valuation and loss control organizations, and advisory groups.

15) Electronic data interchange (EDI) allows different systems to interact without human involvement and is defined as a standards-driven technology for high volume B2B (business to business) e-business transaction exchange, linking application systems across enterprises, so that a transaction on one system at one company generates a like transaction on a system at another company.

16) In an EDI-based transaction, different systems at different organizations, or within the same organization, can “talk” to each other in a common format, eliminating the need for human involvement at multiple stages in the process.

17) The correct answer choice is “B”.

18) Object–The initial word, identifies the entity–for example the person, place, thing, process, or concept–that has the attribute in question.

    Property term–The second part of a data element name, specifies the property, or characteristic, of the entity to which the data element refers.

    Representation or class term–The third part of a data element name, is used to categorize a data element into a particular data type. It represents the general purpose or use of the data element and should always be the last word in a data element name.

19) Codes are to be designed to achieve an acceptable level of credibility for the information collected by using simple language and the avoidance of complex coding structures. When the best possible configuration of fields or codes is considered not conducive to quality data, procedures must be improved to enhance quality.

20) Rule 17–Avoidance of Redundancy.

21) The correct answer choice is “A”.

22) Rule 21–Reevaluation of Data Elements and Rule 22–Reevaluation of Standards and Guidelines.

23) The correct answer choice is “D”.

24) Data dictionary typically includes the data element names, a description of the information provided by each data element, and any associated business and/or technical metadata required by internal and external users of the system.

25) Data standards are imposed by regulators; some reflect traditional business practices; some have been developed by industry groups through open discussion and consensus.

    Areas in which standards exist include the following:

- Terminology
- Coverage and forms
- Accounting practices
- Solvency requirements
- Market conduct
- Rating and pricing
- Business processes
- Data quality and consistency
- Data exchange

26) Standards are developed by standards development organizations (SDOs) – SDOs are voluntary organizations. SDOs develop standards through collaboration and negotiation. Organizations that create standards in this open, consultative manner are not static. They spend considerable time maintaining current standards and attempting to coordinate them with other existing standards.

27) Initiate the Project; Mobilize the Work Group; Draft the Standard; Ballot the Standard; Gain Final Approval; and Maintain the Standard.

28) Insurance rate regulation focuses on achieving three goals: Rates should be adequate to maintain insurer solvency to protect consumers; Rates should not be excessive; coverage should be reasonably affordable; and Rates should not discriminate unfairly, although they may vary based on risk factors.

29) To deter insurers from engaging in unfair business practices, regulators periodically review their underwriting and claims settlement procedures, and verify that the rates and forms used are those that have received regulatory approval where such approval is required.

30) NAIC stands for National Association of Insurance Commissioners (NAIC). The primary reason for insurance regulation is to protect consumers. In order to ensure that appropriate coverage is available and reasonably priced, and that legitimate claims are fairly and promptly paid, regulators such as NAIC focus on three areas: Insurer solvency; Market conduct; and Ratemaking.

31) International Organization for Standardization (ISO) is the world's largest SDO. ISO standards are crafted by technical committees populated by subject matter experts from industry, non-governmental organizations, government agencies, and others who have been recommended by ISO members. ISO 8000 standard focuses on data quality.

32) The mission of the American National Standards Institute (ANSI) is "To enhance the global competitiveness of U.S. business and the U.S. quality of life by promoting and facilitating voluntary consensus standards and conformity assessment systems, and safeguarding their integrity." ANSI is not an SDO as such. One important element of implementing International Organization for Standardization (ISO) standards is conformity assessment. This is the process of determining whether an organization's products or services actually comply with the requirements outlined in a particular ISO standard.

33) There are three methods of assessing conformity: Certification, testing, and inspection.

34) The phase of an underwriting cycle wherein the desire for increased market share drives some insurers to relax underwriting standards and lower rates. To remain competitive, other insurers follow suit, and

consumers find insurance coverage easy to obtain at acceptable premiums, resulting in, what is termed as a "soft market". Conversely, when premiums rise, called a "Hard market", some consumers unable to afford coverage, or to obtain coverage at any price may cause instability in business continuation.

35) Insurers must be financially stable in order to meet their obligations to policyholders. Regulators establish financial standards that insurers are required to meet, for example minimum capitalization. They review insurers' financial statements and perform tests to identify insurers with potential solvency problems.

36) The correct answer choice is "A".

Data and Information Integrity

Educational Objectives

Upon completion of this assignment, you should be able to:

1. Define data integrity and information integrity.
2. Describe the basic components of a relational database.
3. Describe the problems lack of data integrity can cause an organization.
4. Describe the goals of maintaining data integrity.
5. Explain the principles of transaction management.
6. Explain the strategies, generations, and functions of maintaining data integrity.
7. Identify the types of integrity constraints that should be considered prior to data validation.
8. Describe the phenomenon of disparate data and the cycle that perpetuates it.
9. Describe how the cycle of disparate data can be broken.
10. Explain the concepts of an integrated data resource and common data architecture.

For each assignment, define or describe each of the Key Terms and Concepts and answer each of the Review and Discussion Questions.

Key Terms and Concepts

Data integrity

Information integrity

Relation

Record

Data set or Entity set

Field

Primary key

Foreign key

Silent data corruption

ACID Properties ***(Atomicity, Consistency, Isolation, and Durability)***

Data normalization

Business rule

Business rule management systems (BRMS)

Data validation techniques

Data validation

Constraint

Referential integrity

Generation data group

Generation

Disparate data

Data resource integration

Enterprise data architecture

Review Questions

1) Define data integrity and information integrity.

2) Describe the basic components of a relational database.

3) Describe the problems a lack of data integrity can cause an organization.

4) List the data management activities aimed at enhancing and maintaining data integrity.

5) Explain the principles of transaction management.

6) List and briefly describe the types of integrity constraints that should be considered prior to data validation.

7) Which of the following is NOT a type of data integrity constraint in general use?

   A. Check constraints.

   B. Null constraints.

   C. Unique constraints.

   D. Foreign key constrains.

8) Describe how the cycle of disparate data can be broken.

9) Which of the following statement, or statements, best describes disparate data?

I. Data are in different formats, in different systems, implemented in different ways on different platforms.

II. Data are locked in information silos and are not generally accessible across the organization.

III. Data are homogeneous across an enterprise.

IV. Existing data may not be trusted so data are created or acquired.

A. II and III.

B. I, II, and III.

C. Only I.

D. I, II, and IV.

10) Explain the concepts of an integrated data resource and common data architecture.

11) Which of the following statements best define data integrity?

I. The data are trustworthy.

II. The data have not been breached.

III. The data are uncorrupted.

IV. The data are inaccessible.

A. III.

B. II and IV.

C. I and II.

D. None of these.

12) Accurate, complete, consistent, and valid are characteristics of which of the following:

A. Data integration.

B. Information integrity.

C. Transaction management.

D. Data validation.

13) Which of the following issues may occur within an organization due to lack of data integrity?

A. System crashes.

B. Regulatory intervention.

C. Lost credibility.

D. All of the above.

14) Which of the following costs are most associated with system downtime caused by data integrity issues?

A. Data restoration.

B. In-force business loss.

C. Hardware upgrade expenses.

D. Software update expenses.

15) Name the term for undetected damage to data integrity and explain why this is an issue.

16) The properties that every transaction should have in order for systems to automatically manage transactions in a way that helps preserve data integrity are:

A. Atomicity, consistency, isolation, durability.

B. Atomicity, cognitive, informational, detailed.

C. Atomicity, consistency, informational, detailed.

D. Atomicity, cognitive, isolation, durability.

17) List the steps ACID transactions typically involve to ensure atomicity, consistency, isolation, and durability.

18) List the techniques data management professionals can use to help ensure data integrity.

19) The objective of data normalization is to:

A. Limit some particular aspect of the organization's operation.

B. Confirm that something meets requirements, follows rules, and conforms to standards.

C. Limit the values that can be inserted into columns in a table.

D. Store one fact in one place.

20) Describe the rules on which referential integrity relies.

21) The cycle by which data that is not documented or integrated, that cannot be accessed or trusted, resulting in the creation or acquisition of data rather than using the existing data is known as which of the following?

A. Disparate Data Cycle.

B. Redundant Data Cycle.

C. Integrated Data Cycle.

D. Validated Data Cycle.

22) The process that transforms an organization's various disparate data resources into a homogeneous data resource that exists at the operational level rather than simply within a data warehouse or federation is known as which of the following?

A. Data integration.

B. Enterprise data architecture.

C. Data resource integration.

D. Generation data group.

23) Data resource integration results in which of the following?

A. Disparate data.

B. Data that can be shared and accessed across the enterprise.

C. Data locked in information silos.

D. Data that is scrubbed, transformed, and stored for operational and analytical purposes.

24) Which of the following is an essential element of data resource integration?

A. A common, enterprise-wide data architecture.

B. A relational database.

C. A virtual data federation.

D. A physical data warehouse.

25) Describe how the data validation methods can be implemented.

Discussion Questions

NOTE: The below questions are intended to continue to challenge you to test your knowledge of the required reading by applying what you have studied to real-life situations.

No suggested answers are provided at the end of the assignment for these types of open discussion questions. Answers may vary by student and will depend on their organization's culture, resources, and processes!

1) Identify a data integrity issue that you have experienced, what was the cause, how was it rectified?

2) Discuss the techniques your organization uses to ensure data integrity.

3) Discuss the steps your organization has taken to break the disparate data cycle.

Answers to Assignment 4 Questions

NOTE: These answers are provided to give students a basic understanding of acceptable types of responses. They are often not the only valid answers and are not intended to provide an exhaustive response to the questions.

Key Terms and Concepts

Data integrity: The extent to which data are trustworthy, meaning that they are complete, accurate, consistent, and uncorrupted.

Information integrity: The extent to which information is accurate, complete, consistent, and valid.

Relation: The file or table that introduces some fundamental database concepts.

Record: The collection of information about an entity.

Data set or Entity set: A collection of similar entities represented as numbers, characters, symbols, or images of a particular entity.

Field: The point at which a row and column intersect in a database.

Primary key: A unique identifier of data, for example the Employee ID Number.

Foreign key: When a primary key from one entity appears in another entity, it is referred to as a foreign key.

Silent data corruption: Undetected damage to data integrity, which often goes unrecognized because they resemble good data.

ACID Properties (*Atomicity, Consistency, Isolation, and Durability*): Properties of Atomicity, Consistency, Isolation, Durability. It is the Database designers' principle or technique to manage transactions to preserve data integrity.

- Atomicity: a database property that all steps in a transaction must complete successfully.
- Consistency: database transaction must be consistent or reconcilable.
- isolation: when multiple transactions are processed concurrently, each transaction must be completed as if it were in isolation.
- durability: the property that database transaction is completed, in committed state and recoverable.

Data normalization: A method for increasing the quality of database design by including only attributes of the primary key in each entity.

Business rule: A formal statement that stipulates what an organization will or will not do to define or limit a particular aspect of the organizations' operations.

Business rule management systems (BRMS): A management system to separate business rules from the rest of an application to allow business managers to modify business rules without making changes to the application.

Data validation techniques: Techniques to verify data validation is accurate. Some techniques are:

- Data type validation checks whether the data in a field are of the type expected.
- Allowed character checks verify whether the characters entered are among those allowed or required.
- Range checking involves determining whether the data in a field are within the expected range.
- Code checking verifies that a code entered in a field is valid.
- Complex validation can involve a combination of simple data validation methods with the addition of more complex processing.

Data validation: The process of determining and confirming that something meets requirements, follows rules, and conforms to standards.

Constraint: Constraints help preserve data integrity by controlling or limiting the values that can be inserted into columns in a table. Constraint types:

- Check constraints specify the acceptable format of data in a column.
- Not null constraints do not allow a field to be left blank.
- Unique constraints ensure that unique values remain so.
- Primary key constraints are essentially a combination of not null constraints and unique constraints that apply to the primary key column in a table.
- Foreign key constraints ensure that the value in a foreign key column in one table matches a primary key in another table.

Referential integrity: Referential integrity means that every foreign key in a table has an identical primary key in that same table or another table.

Generation data group: A collection of sequential automatic backups of a particular data set.

Generation: An automatic backup of a particular data set.

Disparate data: Data collected, created, and acquired from disparate sources. Heterogeneous data that is dissimilar in structure, format, or meaning.

Data resource integration: The process of making disparate data across an enterprise homogeneous and ensuring that they remain so and are adequate to meet both present and future business information requirements.

Enterprise data architecture: The formal, comprehensive data process architecture to provide a common context within which organizations develop an integrated data resource across an enterprise; a blueprint for aligning IT functions with the organization's business strategy.

Review Questions

1) Data integrity is the extent to which data are trustworthy, meaning that they are complete, accurate, consistent, and uncorrupted. Information integrity is the extent to which information is accurate, complete, consistent, and valid.

2) Relational databases are collections of files with rows and columns like a spreadsheet. In a relational database, data is collected into tables (called relations). A table represents some class of objects that are important to an organization; for example, employees, customers, or stores. Each table is built of columns and rows. Each column represents some attribute of the object represented by the table. Each row represents an instance of the object represented by the table.

3) A lack of data integrity leads to a lack of information integrity. This may lead to some or all of the following: system crashes, cost of system downtime, silent data corruption, lost credibility, inappropriate business decisions, lost confidence in data, and regulatory intervention.

4) The goals of data integrity management activities are to:

- Ensure the quality and integrity of the information derived from data.
- Prevent system crashes resulting from data corruption.
- Reduce the direct and indirect costs of system downtime.
- Recognize "dirty data" promptly to prevent silent data corruption.
- Protect the organization's credibility with stakeholders and others.
- Support appropriate business planning and decision making.
- Enhance confidence in the trustworthiness of data.
- Comply with regulatory requirements.

5) Companies in the insurance industry manage many transactional activities such as processing policies; endorsements; claims, accepting and making payments; and a variety of other operations. Transaction management ensures that these types of transactions process reliably. A common approach to transaction management is to allow systems to automatically manage transactions in a way that helps preserve data integrity. This approach involves ensuring that all transactions have four specific properties: atomicity, consistency, isolation, and durability.

6) The types of integrity constraints that should be considered prior to data validation are:

- Check constraints specify the acceptable format of data in a column.
- Not null constraints do not allow a field to be left blank.
- Unique constraints ensure that unique values remain so.
- Primary key constraints are essentially a combination of not null constraints and unique constraints that apply to the primary key column in a table. They ensure that each record has a primary key and each is unique.
- Foreign key constraints ensure that the value in a foreign key column in one table matches a primary key in another table.

7) The correct answer choice is "B".

8) An effective way of breaking the Disparate Data Cycle is through the development of an integrated data resource with common data architecture.

9) The correct answer choice is "D".

10) Integrated data resource can be achieved by transforming various disparate data resources into a homogeneous data resource that exists at the operational level rather than simply within a data warehouse or federation. Common data architecture is maintaining a blueprint for aligning IT functions with business strategy. Both integrated data resource and common data architecture are measures to break disparate data cycle and establishing data integrity.

11) The correct answer choice is "C".

12) The correct answer choice is “B”.

13) The correct answer choice is “D”.

14) The correct answer choice is “B”.

15) Undetected damage to data integrity is referred to as Silent Data Corruption. Dirty data can often go unrecognized because they resemble good data. When undetected for any length of time, the corruption can infect backups and spread to other systems, significantly increasing the time, effort, and cost to restore data integrity.

16) The correct answer choice is “A”.

17) In order to ensure atomicity, consistency, isolation, and durability, ACID transactions typically involve the following steps:

- Document the transaction request in a transaction log.
- Obtain write locks on all the data elements involved in the transaction.
- Insert the new values into the appropriate fields.
- Move the changes from temporary to permanent storage (i.e. analogous to “Save”).
- Update the transaction log to flag the transaction as completed.

18) To help ensure data integrity, data management professionals can use the following techniques:

- Normalizing data
- Defining business rules
- Validating data
- Using constraints
- Imposing referential integrity
- Using generation data groups

19) The correct answer choice is “D”.

20) A foreign key cannot be added to an entity unless it exists as a primary key in another table. A row, or record, cannot be deleted from a table if foreign keys in other tables refer to that record. And finally, a record cannot be added to a table unless the foreign key for that record matches a primary key in the table to which the foreign key refers.

21) The correct answer choice is “A”.

22) The correct answer choice is “C”.

23) The correct answer choice is “B”.

24) The correct answer choice is “A”.

25) Data validation techniques can be implemented in several different ways. For example, the user interface can prompt users to complete required fields or format their input in a specific way. Data validation can also be accomplished through the application itself or through the use of database constraints.

Metadata and Metadata Management

Educational Objectives

Upon completion of this assignment, you should be able to:

1. Define metadata and explain their importance.
2. Discuss the challenges of managing metadata.
3. Define semantics and taxonomy.
4. Identify the major types of metadata classification.
5. List the advantages of having high quality metadata and the disadvantages of having poor quality metadata.
6. Explain data lineage and describe how it is useful to the metadata user.
7. Describe how different types of data users employ metadata.
8. Explain the rationale for implementing a metadata strategy.
9. Describe the challenges in implementing a metadata strategy.
10. Explain the role of metadata repositories.
11. Discuss the value of an enterprise metadata repository.
12. Contrast centralized vs. autonomous metadata.
13. List the characteristics of an enterprise metadata repository.
14. Describe metadata user requirements, architecture, and standards.
15. Discuss the challenges of implementing and managing an enterprise metadata repository.
16. Discuss the considerations for buying versus building a metadata repository.

For each assignment, define or describe each of the Key Terms and Concepts and answer each of the Review and Discussion Questions.

Key Terms and Concepts

Metadata

Metadata management

Semantics

Taxonomy

Business metadata

Technical metadata

Operational metadata

Process metadata

Data stewardship metadata

Descriptive metadata

Structural metadata

Administrative metadata

Data lineage

Meta-tags

Metadata repository

Metamodel

Review Questions

1) Discuss the challenges of managing metadata.

2) Describe some of the challenges in implementing a metadata strategy.

3) Explain the role of metadata repositories.

4) Discuss the value of an enterprise metadata repository.

5) Contrast centralized vs. autonomous metadata.

6) List the characteristics of an enterprise metadata repository.

7) Which of the following statements best describe the importance of metadata?

   A. They describe the content, quality, condition, and other attributes of the data.

   B. They put data in context, reveal their meaning, and make them accessible and usable.

   C. They serve as the foundation for data quality, data profiling, and data use.

   D. All of the above.

8) Which of the following statements does NOT describe the importance of metadata?

   A. They classify data in a simple list.

   B. They put data in context, reveal their meaning, and make them accessible and usable.

   C. They serve as the foundation for data quality, data profiling, and data use.

   D. They describe the content, quality, condition, and other attributes of the data.

9) Identify some of the sources for insurance metadata.

10) Which of the following can be a challenge faced when managing metadata?

A. There are a variety of tools to capture and store metadata.

B. Metadata can be found in various locations throughout an enterprise.

C. Users access the metadata through a single portal.

D. Most organizations have a sufficient number of individuals with the skill set to manage metadata.

11) Which of the following processes of defining and documenting an organization is helped by semantics?

A. Underwriting policies.

B. IT infrastructure.

C. Business and technical terms.

D. Rules and guidelines.

12) Simple lists, hierarchical classification, and faceted classification are all methods of which of the following?

A. Semantics.

B. Operational metadata.

C. Structural metadata.

D. Taxonomy.

13) The date and time a file was last updated is an example of which type of metadata classification?

A. Business metadata.

B. Process metadata.

C. Operational metadata.

D. All of the above.

14) Business, technical, operational, process, and data stewardship metadata are typically associated with which of the following?

A. Structured data.

B. Unstructured data.

C. Value chain.

D. Authority or responsibility.

15) Metadata about unstructured data are characterized as which of the following?

I. Descriptive.

II. Technical/Structural.

III. Business.

IV. Administrative.

A. I and III.

B. III.

C. I, II, and III.

D. I, II, and IV.

16) List the characteristics of good quality metadata.

17) List the characteristics of poor quality metadata.

18) Which of the following statements does NOT describe the advantages of having good quality metadata?

A. The organization understands and has confidence in its data and information.

B. The organization's information is duplicated or reworked.

C. The organization communicates through a common vocabulary.

D. The organization can use and reuse its data.

19) Which of the following includes the processes, transformations, and validations the data have undergone?

A. Data standards.

B. Data model.

C. Data retention.

D. Data lineage.

20) Which of the following statements best describe the usefulness of data lineage?

I. Organizations can demonstrate the accuracy and integrity of their financial and statutory reporting.

II. Highlights the downstream impact of system or process changes.

III. Organizations are better able to protect sensitive and confidential information.

IV. Can reduce data collection, storage, and dispersal costs.

A. I only.

B. I, II, III, and IV.

C. I and II only.

D. I, II and IV only.

21) How does metadata management alleviate senior management concerns of inaccurate financial reports or breaches in confidentiality?

22) Which statement best describes how metadata ensures that actuaries and other analysts have the right data for analysis?

A. They support compliance with reporting requirements.

B. They reduce the cost of collection, storage, and dispersal.

C. They provide their characteristics, where they came from, and the transformations they have undergone.

D. They identify profitable or unprofitable coverages or lines of business.

23) Metadata that links data about prospects and customers across systems internally and externally supports which area of an organization?

A. Statistical and Regulatory Compliance.

B. Marketing.

C. Information Technology.

D. Claims.

24) Which statement best describes a metadata strategy?

A. It is formulated at the same organizational level as other strategic plans.

B. It establishes a framework for meeting future information needs.

C. It increases recognition of the importance of data and metadata quality.

D. All of the above.

25) The enhanced ability to derive information from operational data is a benefit of which of the following?

A. Metadata strategy.

B. Data lineage.

C. Semantics.

D. Metadata repository.

26) Which of the following challenges could an organization face when developing and implementing a metadata strategy?

I. Lack of executive support.

II. Few resources with the appropriate skills.

III. Business users are engaged in the project.

IV. Ongoing maintenance costs are needed.

A. I, II, and IV.

B. III and IV.

C. I, II, and III.

D. II and III.

27) An index in a table is an example of which of the following?

A. Centralized repository metadata.

B. Metadata architecture.

C. Metadata classification.

D. Autonomous metadata.

28) Which of the following statements best describe autonomous metadata?

A. Data are used locally for a unique purpose with no value to the organization.

B. Data requires standardization.

C. Data are available for general use.

D. Data are integrated.

29) The three most common architectural approaches to shared metadata are:

A. Centralized, Distributed, Integrated.

B. Integrated, Hybrid, Distributed.

C. Centralized, Distributed, Hybrid.

D. Centralized, Extensible, Distributed.

30) Metadata that are always current and valid without the need for replication and synchronization is an advantage of which type of metadata repository architecture?

A. Centralized.

B. Distributed.

C. Extensible.

D. Integrated.

31) The need for additional software and IT resources to extract metadata from the repository is a disadvantage of which type of metadata repository architecture?

A. Centralized.

B. Distributed.

C. Hybrid.

D. Integrated.

32) How do standards assist an organization when building a custom metadata repository?

33) What should an organization look for, with regards to standards, when purchasing a metadata repository tool?

34) Which of the following is NOT a challenge of implementing and managing a metadata repository?

   A. Requires knowledgeable individuals with specific skill sets.

   B. Repository management products typically require customization.

   C. Determining which metadata to include and populating the repository.

   D. Starting on a smaller scale and growing the repository gradually.

35) True or false, data stewardship metadata provides rules about who has the authority or responsibility for creating, reading, updating, or deleting data?

Discussion Questions

NOTE: The below questions are intended to continue to challenge you to test your knowledge of the required reading by applying what you have studied to real-life situations.

No suggested answers are provided at the end of the assignment for these types of open discussion questions. Answers may vary by student and will depend on their organization's culture, resources, and processes!

1) Identify how metadata are managed within your organization; is it an IT function, managed by a data steward, or some combination of both? And discuss the advantages and disadvantages to using the management model.

2) Give at least two examples of different terms that are used synonymously by different departments or divisions in your organization.

3) Explain how you use metadata in your role at your organization?

4) Identify the architecture type of your organization's metadata repository and discuss the advantages and disadvantages to using this type.

Answers to Assignment 5 Questions

NOTE: These answers are provided to give students a basic understanding of acceptable types of responses. They are often not the only valid answers and are not intended to provide an exhaustive response to the questions.

Key Terms and Concepts

Metadata: Metadata are "data about data". Metadata, which is the business and technical information about an organization's data, describes the content, quality, condition, and other attributes of the data, and the structure of the database such that it helps put data in context, revealing their meaning and making them accessible.

Metadata management: The preparation, definition, organization, managed access, and maintenance of an organization's metadata.

Semantics: In the context of data management, semantics is the process of clearly defining and documenting the business and technical terms used within an organization.

Taxonomy: In data management, taxonomy is a classification system in which items can be classified in simple lists, hierarchically, or when an item needs to be categorized in a variety of ways, using a faceted classification method.

Business metadata: Non-technical metadata elements to define data and their attributes in business terms with meaning to business users of the data.

Technical metadata: Metadata used by an organization's systems to manipulate data resources to meet business needs.

Operational metadata: Metadata to describe the data's availability, movement from source to target systems, timeliness, and usage.

Process metadata: Metadata with a focus on the business value chain providing information about the business process.

Data stewardship metadata: Metadata about data stewards and data stewardship processes, including rules about who has the authority or responsibility for creating, reading, updating, or deleting data.

Descriptive metadata: Metadata about the content of unstructured data that help locate required data.

Structural metadata: Structural metadata, also called technical metadata, describes the format, internal structure, and organization of data.

Administrative metadata: Metadata that relate to the management of unstructured data resources, such as a document's creation date, copyright information, or retention requirements.

Data lineage: The history of a particular data element from its original creation or acquisition to its current or future form; includes all of the processes, transformations, manual interventions and validations the data have undergone and identifies the various systems through which the data may have flowed.

Meta-tags: Meta-tags are words that are tagged to items on the web.

Metadata repository: Metadata repository is a database and the software used to capture, manage, and access metadata. It serves as a data warehouse for an organization to collect, integrate, standardize, consolidate, organize, control, and store its metadata and make them available for shared general use.

Metamodel: A data model for a metadata database that helps an organization understand its metadata requirements.

Review Questions

1) Metadata are typically found in various forms and locations throughout an enterprise, particularly in organizations of a variety of sizes, or those that have been involved in mergers or acquisitions. Metadata can be formal, structured and documented, or informal and unstructured. This makes managing metadata challenging.

2) Some of the challenges in implementing a metadata strategy are: cost to establish, executive support, organization's cultural acceptance, complexities of reengineering internal IT functions, and ongoing effort and costs.

3) A metadata repository is a database and software used to capture, manage and access metadata. Like a data warehouse, a metadata repository is where an organization collects, integrates, standardizes, consolidates, organizes, controls, and stores its metadata, and makes them available for shared general use.

4) Enterprise metadata repository can result in reduced operating costs, increased productivity, improved utilization of resources; and enhanced delivery of products and services.

5) Centralized metadata are where all of the data are in one single repository to ensure consistency, integration, and control, and facilitate the sharing of metadata across the organization.

   Autonomous metadata are data which does not need to be shared and centralization would provide no benefit. Including autonomous metadata in the repository would significantly and unnecessarily increase the scope and cost of the repository implementation project with little or no benefit to the organization.

6) An enterprise metadata repository: Contains metadata; Contains definitions of the metadata; Stores information in the database; Defines its contents by one or more metamodels; Provides extensibility; Integrates its contents; Facilitates access to metadata; and Facilitates population of the repository.

7) The correct answer choice is "D".

8) The correct answer choice is "A".

9) Sources of insurance metadata include insurers' policy administration systems, billing systems, claims systems, information and reporting systems, and the content management systems used for storing unstructured data. Other sources of insurance metadata include insurance regulators and data collection organizations (i.e. with respect to regulatory reporting requirements), and other third parties. Data architecture activities, such as data modeling and extract, transform and load (ETL), also produce metadata.

10) The correct answer choice is "B".

11) The correct answer choice is "C".

12) The correct answer choice is "D".

13) The correct answer choice is "C".

14) The correct answer choice is "A".

15) The correct answer choice is "D".

16) Accurate, Complete, Current, Consistent and have Integrity.

17) Insufficient, Inconsistent, Ambiguous, Redundant, and Disparate.

18) The correct answer choice is "B".

19) The correct answer choice is "D".

20) The correct answer choice is "B".

21) Metadata management helps alleviate concerns in these areas by providing the data's full lineage, and defining the levels of privacy needed for each piece of data.

22) The correct answer choice is "C".

23) The correct answer choice is "B".

24) The correct answer choice is "D".

25) The correct answer choice is "A".

26) The correct answer choice is "A".

27) The correct answer choice is "D".

28) The correct answer choice is "A".

29) The correct answer choice is "C".

30) The correct answer choice is "B"

31) The correct answer choice is "A".

32) Using standards can reduce the amount of work associated with the repository's design and architecture.

33) If an organization decides to purchase a metadata repository tool, it is best to find one that is compliant with the latest technical standards, has an open architecture to allow customization, and has been based on common metamodel standards.

34) The correct answer choice is "D".

35) True.

Reference Data and Master Data Management

Educational Objectives

Upon completion of this assignment, you should be able to:

1. Define reference data.
2. Describe the various types of reference data and value domains. Provide examples of each.
3. Define master data.
4. Describe the various types of master data. Provide an example of each.
5. Describe the differences between reference data and master data.
6. Define the concept of golden records and describe their importance.
7. Describe the most common drivers of reference data and master data management.
8. Describe the activities in implementing reference data and master data management.
9. Define entity resolution.
10. List and define the types of matching rules and their uses.
11. Describe the challenges in implementing reference data and master data management.
12. Explain the principles of implementing reference data and master data management functions into an organization.
13. Explain how reference data and master data contribute to data integrity and quality.

For each assignment, define or describe each of the Key Terms and Concepts and answer each of the Review and Discussion Questions.

Key Terms and Concepts

Reference data

Master data

Transactional data

Golden record

Reference data management (RDM)

Controlled vocabulary

System of record

Master data management (MDM)

Inference engine

Affiliation management

Entity resolution

Duplicate identification matching rules

Match-merge rules

Match-link rules

Operational data store (ODS)

Review Questions

1) Which statement best defines reference data?

   A. Data that are not updated or altered by business applications.

   B. Data about specific events.

   C. Data about those things that are essential to an organization.

   D. Data about data.

2) Describe the various types of reference data and value domains. Provide examples of each.

3) Data that are commonly stored in look-up or code tables which define the domain, or set of valid values for a data element, best describes which of the following?

   A. Metadata.

   B. Master data.

   C. Reference data.

   D. Transactional data.

4) A table used to determine an employee's work status and benefit eligibility falls under which of the following reference table structure categories?

   A. Taxonomy.

   B. Mapping table.

   C. Code list.

   D. Multiple attributes of a single entity type.

5) Which of the following are considered a type of reference data structure?

I. Taxonomies.

II. Code lists.

III. Mapping tables.

IV. General ledger.

A. I and IV.

B. I, II, and III.

C. I, II and IV.

D. All of these choices.

6) An insurer's master data would include data about which of the following?

I. Products and services.

II. Geographic territories.

III. Codes and descriptions.

IV. Competitors.

A. IV only.

B. I, III, and IV.

C. I, II, and IV.

D. All of these choices.

7) Data in general ledger accounts is an example of which category of master data?

A. Product master data.

B. Geographic master data.

C. Party master data.

D. Financial master data.

8) Data about insurance policies and endorsements best describes which category of master data?

   A. Product master data.

   B. Financial master data.

   C. Party master data.

   D. Geographic master data.

9) Which of the following is NOT a master data category?

   A. Party master data.

   B. Financial master data.

   C. Performance master data.

   D. Product master data.

10) Describe the differences between reference data and master data.

11) Ensuring the accuracy and standardization of information that can be shared among all systems across an organization is a benefit of which of the following?

   A. Controlled vocabulary.

   B. Golden record.

   C. Master data.

   D. System of record.

12) Which of the following is NOT a common driver of reference data and master data management?

   A. Improving data quality and integration across data sources, applications, and technologies.

   B. Providing a consolidated 360-degree view of information for more effective reporting and analytics.

   C. Communicating more effectively through a common vocabulary.

   D. All of the above.

13) Describe the activities in implementing reference data and master data management.

14) Identifying the records that represent the same entity and integrating them into a single representation of that entity is known as which of the following?

   A. Entity management.

   B. Entity matching rules.

   C. Entity identification.

   D. Entity resolution.

15) Which of the following identify the three types of, or approaches to, matching rules?

   A. Duplicate identification, match-merge, match-save.

   B. Match-link, duplicate inference, match-merge.

   C. Match-merge, duplicate identification, match-link.

   D. None of the above.

16) Which of the three types of matching rules runs the risk of unrelated records being inappropriately changed?

    A. Match-merge.

    B. Duplicate identification.

    C. Match-link.

    D. All of the above.

17) How does the use of duplicate identification matching rules prevent records from being incorrectly matched?

18) Describe the challenges in implementing reference data and master data management.

19) Which of the following is NOT a challenge of implementing reference data?

    A. Mapping different types of externally sourced codes.

    B. Different applications often use different reference data internally.

    C. Definitions or categorization of externally sourced reference data may differ.

    D. Identifying the one golden record among multiple, often conflicting records.

20) Using the golden record in all systems across the organization, rather than other, less accurate records is a challenge for which of the following?

    A. Master data management.

    B. Reference data management.

    C. Affiliation management.

    D. A and B are correct.

21) List the principles of implementing reference data and master data management functions into an organization.

22) A successful MDM/RDM initiative focuses on which of the following?

A. Products and services.

B. Applications and business processes.

C. Evaluating customer's needs.

D. Supporting regulatory compliance.

23) Which of the following best describe how RDM and MDM contribute to data integrity and quality?

A. Ensure accurate data consistent with the organizations business rules.

B. Enhances the quality of the information supporting regulatory compliance.

C. Ensure standardized data.

D. All of the above.

Discussion Questions

NOTE: The below questions are intended to continue to challenge you to test your knowledge of the required reading by applying what you have studied to real-life situations.

No suggested answers are provided at the end of the assignment for these types of open discussion questions. Answers may vary by student and will depend on their organization's culture, resources, and processes!

1) Identify and discuss reference data you use to perform your work. What type of structure or structures are used in this reference data?

2) Give at least two examples of master data within your organization and identify which master data category applies to the data.

3) Discuss some of the benefits you've experience from having access to the golden record. Discuss some instances where not having a golden record or access to the golden record limited your ability to do your job.

Answers to Assignment 6 Questions

NOTE: These answers are provided to give students a basic understanding of acceptable types of responses. They are often not the only valid answers and are not intended to provide an exhaustive response to the questions.

Key Terms and Concepts

Reference data: RDM entails devising codes for, descriptions and definitions of, and relationships among the organization's internally developed and externally sourced reference data for identification or creation of "golden records" of reference data for shared use across an organization.

Master data: Data about those things that are essential to an organization's operations or core business processes.

Transactional data: Data about specific events.

Golden record: A single, complete, accurate, current, and unique set of attributes for an entity.

Reference data management (RDM): RDM entails devising codes for, descriptions and definitions of, and relationships among the organization's internally developed and externally sourced reference data for identification or creation of "golden records" of reference data for shared use across an organization.

Controlled vocabulary: A set of agreed upon terms that are clearly defined, consistently used, and formally managed with rules about how terms are added, modified, or deleted.

System of record: The authoritative source of trustworthy data; the only system authorized to change those data.

Master data management (MDM): The process of defining how master data will be created, maintained, and integrated for general use; implementing appropriate governance, technologies and procedures; and maintaining ongoing master data quality.

Inference engine: The software that applies rules to existing information to infer, or deduce, new information.

Affiliation management: The establishment and maintenance of relationships between master data records.

Entity resolution: The identification of records that represent the same entity and its integration into a single representation of that entity.

Duplicate identification matching rules: master data management rules to devise a specified set of attributes that uniquely identify an entity.

Match-merge rules: master data management rules to compare records based on specified criteria and then automatically merge the data from matching records into a single consolidated record.

Match-link rules: master data management rules to compare other records to a selected record to identify possible matches.

Operational data store (ODS): A vehicle for integrating disparate data from different operational systems.

Review Questions

1) The correct answer choice is "A".
2) Reference data can be categorized based on the way in which they are structured:

- Simple lists of codes and descriptions (example: ISO currency codes).
- Taxonomies indicating relationships (example: NAICS codes).
- Tables revealing multiple attributes of a single entity type (example: Different categories of employees, some who are entitled to benefits and a pension and others of whom are not).
- Code translation or mapping tables (example: State codes – the same data element is expressed differently from system to system [USPS, ISO, FIPS)]).

3) The correct answer choice is "C".

4) The correct answer choice is "D".

5) The correct answer choice is "B".

6) The correct answer choice is "C".

7) The correct answer choice is "D".

8) The correct answer choice is "A".

9) The correct answer choice is "C".

10) Reference data and master data differ in some of the following ways:

- Typically reference data are simpler and lower in volume than master data;
- Reference data tend not to change, or to change slowly. Master data are more complex and far more changeable;
- Reference data are often limited to a relatively small domain whereas for master data, the set of valid values for an attribute can be unlimited;
- While reference data may be developed internally but obtained from external sources; Master data, on the other hand, are generally defined and used internally.

11) The correct answer choice is "B".

12) The correct answer choice is "C".

13) Implementing reference and master data management involves some or all of the following activities:

- Understanding reference and master data integration needs
- Identifying master and reference data sources and contributors
- Defining and maintaining the data integration architecture
- Implementing reference and master data management solutions
- Defining and maintaining matching rules
- Establishing "golden" records
- Defining and maintaining hierarchies and affiliations
- Planning and implementing integration of new data sources
- Replicating and distributing reference and master data
- Managing changes to reference and master data

14) The correct answer choice is “D”.

15) The correct answer choice is “B”.

16) The correct answer choice is “A”.

17) Records that are determined to be matches are not automatically merged. Rather, data managers or business data stewards review them and decide whether or not they are in fact duplicates and should be merged.

18) With reference data, the principle challenge is mapping different types of externally sourced codes and mapping internal codes from different data sources. Also, different applications often use different reference data internally. This adds to the challenge of reference data management because of the time and effort involved in mapping and reconciling codes from various applications. Finally, the definitions or categorization of externally sourced reference data may differ. In the case of master data management, the principle challenges lie in identifying the one “golden record” from among multiple, often conflicting records, and then using that record rather than other, less accurate ones in all systems across the organization.

19) The correct answer choice is “D”.

20) The correct answer choice is “A”.

21) The following five principles can help organizations succeed in implementing reference data and master data management initiatives:

- Define your business problem;
- Plan beyond phase one to ensure success;
- To succeed, MDM needs a strong governance program in place;
- Recognize that the most important word in MDM is management;
- Partner with an IT vendor who has significant MDM and information governance experience.

22) The correct answer choice is “B”.

23) The correct answer choice is “D”.

Data and Information Governance

Educational Objectives

Upon completion of this assignment, you should be able to:

1. Define data governance and information governance.
2. Contrast data and information governance.
3. Describe the importance of data and information governance to an organization.
4. Discuss the role of data and information governance within corporate governance.
5. Describe how the data governance function differs from the IT governance function.
6. Describe the activities necessary to achieve effective data governance.
7. Identify the roles in the data governance function.
8. Define and differentiate data stewardship and information stewardship.
9. Describe how data stewardship functions within the data governance roles.
10. Describe how information stewardship functions within the information governance roles.
11. Describe the importance of data and information stewardship.
12. Describe the challenges of implementing a governance program.
13. Differentiate between the responsibilities of business management and IT management related to data governance decisions.

For each assignment, define or describe each of the Key Terms and Concepts and answer each of the Review and Discussion Questions.

Key Terms and Concepts

Information management

Information governance

Corporate governance

Information technology (IT) governance

Business data stewardship

Business information stewardship

Review Questions

1) Contrast data and information governance.

2) Which of the following best defines data governance?

    A. Identifying an organization's information requirements.

    B. Planning, monitoring, and enforcement over the management of data assets.

    C. Complying with regulatory requirements.

    D. Aligning IT strategy with business strategy and optimizing the use of an organization's IT resources.

3) Identifying an organization's information requirements and then planning, defining, organizing, maintaining, and managing the access to the information that meets those requirements is known as which of the following?

   A. Synchronization of data.

   B. Data governance.

   C. Corporate governance.

   D. Information governance.

4) Which of the following is independent of business process or context?

   A. Synchronization of data.

   B. Data governance.

   C. Corporate governance.

   D. Information governance.

5) Information governance is concerned with which of the following?

   I. Complying with regulatory requirements.

   II. Sharing and reusing information effectively.

   III. Timeliness of data.

   IV. Metadata.

   A. I and III.

   B. II and III.

   C. I and II.

   D. III and IV.

6) Which of the following best describe the importance of data governance and information governance to an organization?

   A. They both have a strategic focus.

   B. They establish and ensure "one version of the truth".

   C. They involve senior executives who should articulate a goal and guiding principles.

   D. All of the above.

7) What is the role of data and information governance within corporate governance?

8) Ensuring the accuracy and integrity of an organization's financial information is how data and information governance supports which of the following?

   A. Data quality management.

   B. IT governance.

   C. Corporate governance.

   D. Data security management.

9) How does the data governance function differ from the IT governance function?

10) List the five elements of IT governance.

11) Which of the following is NOT a goal of IT governance?

A. Meet strategic objectives while minimizing IT risks.

B. Establish metrics for measuring IT performance.

C. Establish principles and policies for managing IT resources.

D. Determine the impact of system changes on data.

12) List some of the activities necessary to achieve effective data governance.

13) Which of the following are the responsibilities of a data governance council or committee (DGC)?

I. Approving master data definitions and proposed master data additions or changes.

II. Communicating compliance requirements.

III. Defining data quality standards.

IV. Maintaining data models.

A. I, II, and III.

B. I and IV.

C. I, II, and IV.

D. All of these choices.

14) Which of the following positions has the goal of continuously improving data quality and integration across the enterprise?

A. Chief data officer (CDO).

B. Information technology (IT).

C. Chief data steward.

D. Data manager.

15) What are the responsibilities typically assigned to the data management professional within their data governance role?

16) What is the difference between data stewardship and information stewardship?

17) List the various activities performed by data stewards within data governance.

18) Describe how information stewardship functions within the information governance roles.

19) Which of the following is NOT performed by information stewards within data governance?

A. Supporting the preparation of external reports.

B. Translating data into concise, meaningful, readily understandable information.

C. Identifying data governance platforms and solutions to be purchased by the enterprise.

D. Identifying and communicating data quality issues.

20) What are some of the challenges of implementing a governance program?

21) In data governance decisions, what are the differences between the responsibilities of business management and IT management?

22) In the context of data governance, which of the following is NOT a business management decision?

A. Identifying and recruiting IT leadership.

B. Data integration architecture.

C. Approving capital investments.

D. Developing the organization's data governance model.

23) In the context of data governance, which of the following statements best describe the IT management decisions?

A. They make decisions about technical issues.

B. They make decisions that directly impact the organization's operations.

C. They make decisions regarding the funding of research and development activities.

D. They make decisions regarding changes to the enterprise's master data.

Discussion Questions

NOTE: The below questions are intended to continue to challenge you to test your knowledge of the required reading by applying what you have studied to real-life situations.

No suggested answers are provided at the end of the assignment for these types of open discussion questions. Answers may vary by student and will depend on their organization's culture, resources, and processes!

1) Identify processes in your organization that rely on the collaborative efforts of business management, data management, and IT management.

2) Discuss why executive sponsorship is the key to a successful data governance program.

3) The assignment discusses governance as it relates to insurance regulation. Briefly list and describe some ways in which governance plays a role.

4) Identify the typical responsibilities of the data management professional in an organization.

Answers to Assignment 7 Questions

NOTE: These answers are provided to give students a basic understanding of acceptable types of responses. They are often not the only valid answers and are not intended to provide an exhaustive response to the questions.

Key Terms and Concepts

Information management: Information management involves identifying an organization's information requirements and then planning, defining, organizing, maintaining, and managing access to high quality, relevant information that meets those requirements.

Information governance: Information governance encompasses the activities and technologies that organizations employ to maximize the value of their information while minimizing associated risks and costs.

Corporate governance: The set of principles and policies an organization develops and implements in an attempt to balance the various interests of its many stakeholders.

Information technology (IT) governance: IT governance objective is to maximize the value of investment in IT by aligning IT strategy with business strategy and optimizing the use of an organization's IT resources.

Business data stewardship: The formal, specifically assigned accountability for ensuring effective control and use of non-technical data assets.

Business information stewardship: The formal, specifically assigned accountability for ensuring effective control and use of non-technical information assets.

Review Questions

1) Information governance encompasses the activities and technologies that organizations employ to maximize the value of their information while minimizing associated risks and costs, whereas data governance is the exercise of authority, control, and shared decision-making (planning, monitoring, and enforcement) over the management of data assets.

2) The correct answer choice is "B".

3) The correct answer choice is "D".

4) The correct answer choice is "B".

5) The correct answer choice is "C".

6) The correct answer choice is "D".

7) Corporate governance is the set of principles and policies an organization develops and implements to balance the interests of its many stakeholders. Effective data and information governance assist corporate governance by supporting the board of directors, shareholders, management, employees, customers, suppliers, government, and the community, and stipulates controls to ensure accuracy of financial information.

8) The correct answer choice is "C".

9) The objective of IT governance is to maximize the value of investment in IT by aligning IT strategy with business strategy and optimizing the use of an organization's IT resources. All the same, data governance has a strategic focus to articulate the goal and guiding principles to manage the implementation of IT governance based on the size, complexity, and culture of the organization.

10) Strategic alignment, value delivery, resource management, risk management, and performance measures.

11) The correct answer choice is "D".

12) Effective data governance provides a foundation on which to base some of the following activities:

- Develop a data strategy to align data management with business needs, and improve and maintain data quality, integrity, security, and access.
- Create data policies that broadly outline what the organization will do in support of the data strategy.
- Define and approve an enterprise data model and enterprise data architecture.
- Create data standards, guidelines, and procedures that specify how the organization will implement its data policies.
- Develop procedures and controls to ensure, monitor, and document compliance with legal and regulatory obligations.
- Establish channels and procedures for identifying and resolving issues related to data.
- Identify, plan, introduce, and manage the organizational and cultural changes necessary to effectively implement the data strategy.
- Consult with IT management to determine the full range of data management and related services the organization requires and plan for required staffing and funding.
- Determine an appropriate method to estimate the tangible and intangible value of the organization's data assets.
- Communicate and promote the value of data assets and the importance of effective data governance.

13) The correct answer choice is "A".

14) The correct answer choice is "A".

15) Ensuring that master data are appropriately documented; Leading efforts to establish data standards; Confirming data quality and data lineage; Supporting data development and associated testing and user acceptance activities; Identifying and resolving redundant and inconsistent terminology; Supporting and encouraging the correction of data quality problems; and Supporting and encouraging the correction of data quality problems.

16) Although the two disciplines overlap in some areas and many of the activities and processes involved are similar, business data stewardship is accountable for ensuring effective control and use of non-technical data assets, while business information stewardship is accountable for ensuring effective control and use of non-technical information assets.

17) Identifying any necessary security requirements; Defining data quality thresholds; Establishing business rules for the data; Identifying and leveraging existing data prior to creating new data, Defining and/or documenting metadata; Verifying data complies with standards; and Ensuring data are used for their intended purpose.

18) Information stewards are subject matter experts in particular fields and are assigned a specific area of responsibility. Depending on the size, structure, and culture of an organization, the information stewardship function can be implemented in a variety of ways:

- A single group performs both data and information governance functions
- A committee or council composed of the individuals that have responsibility for managing information in each of the enterprise's functional areas
- A single organization or functional area responsible for creating all standardized reports, and setting up and managing the facilities for developing information
- An information governance council or committee established along with the data governance council

19) The correct answer choice is "C".

20) Obtaining executive support, maintaining momentum, ensuring adequate staffing and funding, and managing the organizational changes.

21) The responsibilities of IT management are mostly related to translating business rules into data models, maintaining data models, resolving data integration issues, maintaining the metadata repository. The responsibilities of the business management are about such things as devising the organization's business model, identifying and recruiting IT leadership, decisions about capital investments, decisions about research and development activities, and developing the organization's data governance model. IT is accountable for designing and developing, or evaluating and installing, solutions that satisfy data requirements and aligning the enterprise architecture and internal technical standards to the organization's business focus. Operational business leaders determine data requirements; this is not the responsibility of data governance, data management, or IT.

22) The correct answer choice is "B".

23) The correct answer choice is "A".

Information Security

Educational Objectives

Upon completion of this assignment, you should be able to:

1. Describe different classifications of information.
2. Explain the concept of Personally Identifiable Information (PII).
3. Describe the regulatory requirements for handling PII.
4. Define de-identification and explain its role in information security.
5. Describe the implications of poor data and information security for the organization.
6. Describe the various ways in which data and information can be lost and what can be done to prevent their loss.
7. Explain the activities involved in securing organizational data and information.
8. Identify and describe various data and information security controls: administrative, technical, internal, and external.
9. Explain how backup and recovery procedures contribute to data and information security.
10. Define the role and responsibilities of a security governance committee.
11. Describe different roles and responsibilities for ensuring information security.
12. Define the role and responsibilities of data users to ensure information security.
13. Describe how United States federal antitrust laws and regulations apply to the insurance industry.

For each assignment, define or describe each of the Key Terms and Concepts and answer each of the Review and Discussion Questions.

Key Terms and Concepts

External public information

Internal public information

Confidential information

Third party confidential information

Regulated information

Restricted information

Breach notification laws

Privacy laws

Personally identifiable information (PII)

Individually identifiable health information

Pretexting or phishing

De-identification

Encryption

Data masking

Tokenizing

Data and information security

View

Backup and recovery

Review Questions

1) Describe different classifications of information.

2) Explain the concept of Personally Identifiable Information (PII).

3) Describe the regulatory requirements for handling PII.

4) Define de-identification and explain its role in information security.

5) Describe the implications of poor data and information security for the organization.

6) Identify and describe various data and information security controls: administrative, technical, internal, and external.

7) Explain how backup and recovery procedures contribute to data and information security.

8) Define the role and responsibilities of a security governance committee.

9) Define the role and responsibilities of data users to ensure information security.

10) Describe how United States federal antitrust laws and regulations apply to the insurance industry.

11) Which one of the following statements is NOT True?

   A. The Gramm-Leach-Bliley Act, the Health Insurance Protection and Accountability Act (HIPAA), and the NAIC's Principles for Effective Cybersecurity: Insurance Regulatory Guidance all outline how insurers are required to protect the security and confidentiality of the data and information they obtain.

   B. Information can be categorized in a variety of ways: external public, internal public, confidential, regulated, and restricted.

   C. Security audits can help identify exposures to both internal and external risks of data and information loss. They should be undertaken regularly by experienced IT professionals who must be directly responsible for the area being audited.

   D. Internal controls can be either administrative or technical. They are primarily designed to prevent loss resulting from internal sources, although they can also help protect an organization from external threats.

12) True or false, the National Association of Insurance Commissioners (NAIC) is an organization made up of insurance regulators from all 50 states of the United States?

13) True or false, privacy laws in the United States generally attempt to balance the need for individual privacy with the need for efficiency in commercial transactions. In the European Union, on the other hand, privacy is considered a fundamental right and personal information protection laws and regulations are more restrictive than they are in the United States?

Discussion Questions

NOTE: The below questions are intended to continue to challenge you to test your knowledge of the required reading by applying what you have studied to real-life situations.

No suggested answers are provided at the end of the assignment for these types of open discussion questions. Answers may vary by student and will depend on their organization's culture, resources, and processes!

1) Name a legitimate reason for sharing private information.

2) Identify processes in your organization that protect the security of data and information.

3) Give some examples of the implications for an organization when information and data are not properly secured.

Answers to Assignment 8 Questions

NOTE: These answers are provided to give students a basic understanding of acceptable types of responses. They are often not the only valid answers and are not intended to provide an exhaustive response to the questions.

Key Terms and Concepts

External public information: Information made available outside the organization with no restrictions as to its access.

Internal public information: Information that is made readily available for use within an organization.

Confidential information: Any information not specifically identified as public and hence should be kept private.

Third party confidential information: A subset of confidential information and belongs or pertains to another organization that has entrusted it to an organization under a non-disclosure agreement or other contract.

Regulated information: Confidential information for which an authorized regulatory or governmental body has stipulated controls.

Restricted information: Information that is most confidential and highly controlled.

Breach notification laws: Laws requiring private and government organizations in possession of individuals' personal information to notify them when that information has been accessed through a security breach. Breach Notification Laws typically define PII (Personally Identifiable Information).

Privacy laws: Federal government and individual states' laws designed to protect individual privacy.

Personally identifiable information (PII): Any information that can be used to uniquely identify, contact, or locate an individual, either alone or in conjunction with other sources, such as their name, Social Security number, driver's license number, date of birth, place of birth, mother's maiden name, and genetic information.

Individually identifiable health information: Information, including demographic data, that relates to: The individual's past, present, or future physical or mental health or condition; The provision of health care to the individual, or the past, present, or future payment for the provision of health care to the individual.

Pretexting or **phishing:** The practice of obtaining their personal financial information under false pretenses.

De-identification: The removal of any information that might make the remaining information identifiable as relating to a specific individual.

Encryption: The use of algorithms, mathematical operations, to convert data into cipher text, which is not readily comprehensible.

Data masking: Data masking replaces certain data elements with similarly structured but artificial data to protect sensitive information.

Tokenizing: Tokenizing replaces sensitive data, for example a credit card number, with a randomly generated "token".

Data and information security: Data and information security comprises policies and practices that protect data and information against misfortune, attacks, casual accidents, and other potential threats.

View: A presentation of a set of data from one or more physical tables as one logical table. The use of views can restrict access to data in some rows or columns in a table while allowing access to data in the other rows or columns.

Backup and recovery: Backup and recovery is a strategy to keep a copy of programs, files, and databases so that they can be used for recovery in case something happens to the normal master production copy.

Review Questions

1) Information can be classified in a variety of ways, such as external, internal, confidential, regulated, confidential or restricted.

2) Collection and sharing of personal information with advertisers, researchers, and government such as information about a person's internet searches, browsing history, social relationships, medical history, and so forth poses privacy concerns. Federal and state laws have been enacted to prevent invasion of privacy in this manner to control any person from being identified individually through collected data such as first or last name in conjunction with other elements such as social security number, drivers' license, account passwords, etc. Any information that can be used to uniquely identify, contact or locate an individual, when used alone or in conjunction with other sources, can be governed by this group of laws and regulations noted as Personally Identifiable Information laws.

3) Individual jurisdictions enact laws and regulations to control private and government organizations' collection and sharing of Personally Identifiable Information (PII). Any security breach of a person's privacy must be reported as directed in the breach notification laws and privacy laws.

4) In order to manage protecting individuals' personal privacy and yet continue to collect and share information, identifiers that link the data to the specific person must be removed. This process is called de-identification.

5) Following are some of the implications for an organization of poor data and information security:

- Sanctions or penalties due to noncompliance with regulations.
- Disclosure of personally identifiable information about customers, employees, and others.
- Lawsuits by individuals or organizations whose information has been disclosed.
- Damage to the organization's reputation.
- Loss of present and future customers.
- Leakage of information that is sensitive or proprietary to the organization itself.
- Loss of data integrity due to unauthorized or malicious changes to the data.
- Destruction of essential data and information.

6) Organizations implement a variety of controls to help ensure the security of their data and information. Administrative controls are policies and procedures that help ensure unintentional losses of data and information do not occur. Technical controls achieve similar outcomes by using features in hardware and software, and ensuring that employees are only given access to data needed to perform their jobs.

Administrative and technical controls can focus on limiting data and information losses resulting from either internal or external sources.

7) Backup and recovery procedures keep a copy of programs, files, and databases so that they can be used for recovery in case something happens to the normal master production copy. Standard operation procedures for backups help ensure integrity, confidentiality, and availability of backup data.

8) The security governance committee may review the status of the company's computer and network security, and monitor remedial work related to computer and network security incidents and issue. The committee may authorize major projects relating to computer and network security and evaluate their success, approve new or modified information security policies, standards, guidelines, and procedures. The committee may also determine the best methods and practices to achieve information regulatory compliance and review policies and procedures for safeguarding information impacted by external standards and legal requirements.

    - Some roles in the security governance committee may be Chief Information Security Officer (CISO and Security Administrator.

    - CIO - the role of a Chief Information Security Officer (CISO) is to protect the insurance company's data and information by ensuring regulatory compliance and practicing effective risk management.

    - Security Administrator - the security administrator is responsible for establishing, interpreting, implementing, and administering organization-wide IT security policies, standards, guidelines, and procedures.

    - Users - it is important that all employees receive appropriate training in data and information security, and that they clearly understand the implications of a breach in that security.

9) Users of an insurer's data and information, particularly confidential information, are responsible for complying with the organization's security policies and administrative controls. Employees should be trained to identify and promptly report any suspected security incidents, including intrusions and out-of-compliance situations, to the security administrator or to their supervisor.

10) Federal antitrust laws and regulations prohibit certain practices and prohibit insurers from sharing information about:

- Rates presently charged or proposed to be charged by a company
- Restrictions proposed to be placed by a company on the availability of insurance
- Allocation of markets, territories or insureds
- Refusals to deal with third parties
- Profit levels
- Credit terms
- Costs of insurance coverage
- Determinations to quote or not to quote certain classes of business

11) False, the National Association of Insurance Commissioners (NAIC) is an organization made up of insurance regulators from 50 states, the District of Columbia, the Commonwealth of Puerto Rico, and four United States' territories.

12) The correct answer choice is "C".

13) True.

Data Modeling Fundamentals

Educational Objectives

Upon completion of this assignment, you should be able to:

1. Explain the basic concepts underlying data modeling.
2. Define data modeling and describe its importance.
3. Describe the different relationships between entities: one-to-one, one-to-many, many-to-many, recursive.
4. Describe the building blocks of a data model.
5. Describe a database model and how relationships among entities are indicated.
6. Describe the criteria for judging data model quality.

For each assignment, define or describe each of the Key Terms and Concepts and answer each of the Review and Discussion Questions.

Key Terms and Concepts

Composite key ***(sometimes referred to as structured key or concatenated key)***

Data modeling

Conceptual data model (CDM)

Entity-relationship modeling

Logical data model (LDM)

Physical data model (PDM)

One-to-one relationship

One-to-many relationship

Many-to-many relationship

Binary entity relationship

Recursive relationship

Associative entity

Subtype relationship

Supertype relationship

High fidelity data model

Review Questions

1) Explain the basic concepts underlying data modeling.

2) Define data modeling and describe its importance.

3) Describe the different relationships between entities: one-to-one, one-to-many, many-to-many, recursive.

4) Describe the building blocks of a data model.

5) Describe a database model and how relationships among entities are indicated.

6) Describe the criteria for judging data model quality.

7) Which of following statements are true?

I. A physical data model (PDM) is a data model depicting relational tables, columns, foreign key relationships and indexes.

II. A logical data model (LDM) is the data model that accurately and completely depicts the realities of an organization's operations.

III. A conceptual data model (CDM) is created in consultation with business subject matter experts.

IV. When a combination of fields serves as a primary key, it is referred to as the golden key.

A. I and II.

B. II and III.

C. I and III.

D. III and IV.

8) Which one of following statements is NOT true?

A. A particularly well-designed data model is sometimes referred to as "high fidelity".

B. Another feature of a good data model is sometimes referred to as "elegance". An elegant data model is one that is as simple and concise as possible, rather than highly complex.

C. Reference data are data in look-up or code entities that are read but not updated by business applications.

D. In a relational database, not every entity has a primary key. The entities that do not have a primary key are assigned a foreign key.

9) True or false, a relationship between two instances of the same entity type is called a recursive relationship, or self-referencing relationship or unary relationship?

Discussion Questions

NOTE: The below questions are intended to continue to challenge you to test your knowledge of the required reading by applying what you have studied to real-life situations.

No suggested answers are provided at the end of the assignment for these types of open discussion questions. Answers may vary by student and will depend on their organization's culture, resources, and processes!

1) Think about the different entity relationships described in this Assignment. Which ones apply in your organization? Which ones don't? Discuss.

2) Name some of the features of a well-designed data model.

3) Give at least four examples of subtypes and supertypes and how they used in your organization.

Answers to Assignment 9 Questions

NOTE: These answers are provided to give students a basic understanding of acceptable types of responses. They are often not the only valid answers and are not intended to provide an exhaustive response to the questions.

Key Terms and Concepts

Composite key ***(sometimes referred to as structured key or concatenated key)*****:** When a combination of fields serves as a primary key, it is referred to as a composite key or structured key or concatenated key.

Data modeling: A method for determining what data, and what relationships among those data, should be stored in a database.

Conceptual data model (CDM): A conceptual data model (CDM) is created in consultation with business subject matter experts. The process involves determining what data an organization needs to capture or create, and identifying how those data are related to each other.

Entity-relationship modeling: When a data model focuses on entity names and entity relationships, it is referred to as entity-relationship modeling.

Logical data model (LDM): A logical data model (LDM) defines the structures that will be used by the database management system (DBMS).

Physical data model (PDM): A data model depicting relational tables, columns, foreign key relationships and indexes.

One-to-one relationship: A data model relationship when there are only two entities involved.

One-to-many relationship: A data model relationship when one entity is related to two or more entities.

Many-to-many relationship: A data model relationship when multiple entities are involved on both sides of the relationship.

Binary entity relationship: In data model relationship, when only two different types of entities are involved, they are referred to as binary.

Recursive relationship: A relationship between two instances of the same entity type is called a recursive relationship, or self-referencing relationship or unary relationship.

Associative entity: An alternative way for dealing with many-to-many relationships by creating a separate entity to represent the association between two other entities.

Subtype relationship: A way to group a set of entities that share common characteristics.

Supertype relationship: An entity type that has relationships with one or more subtypes.

High fidelity data model: A data model that accurately and completely depicts the realities of an organization's operations.

Review Questions

1) The basic concept of data modeling is about identifying and defining the required entities, identifying the attributes, and exploring and documenting all of the various relationships, possibly creating graphical representation of those relationships.

2) Data modeling is a method for determining what data, and what relationships among those data, should be stored in a database. Data modeling helps organizations understand the organization, document and enforce business rules, facilitate program design and ensure data quality.

3) A data model focuses on entities involved and the relationships between them. Relationships may be one-to-one, one-to-many, many-to-many, or recursive. In a one-to-one relationship, there are only two entities involved; a one-to-many occurs when one entity is related to two or many; many-to-many is when multiple entities are involved on both sides of the relationship; and a relationship between two instances of the same entity type is a recursive or self-referencing relationship.

4) Data models are illustrated using different notations. The basic building blocks in data modeling begin with boxes and lines. Boxes represent entities and lines represent relationships. Boxes, lines, and symbols are used in data modeling to document and define relationships.

5) Using boxes, lines, and symbols, the appropriate symbol is added to each end of the line linking two entity boxes to indicate the type of relationship the entities have. Because there can be more than one relationship between the same two entity types, text is used to clarify the nature of each relationship.

6) A well-crafted data model is complete; is normalized to reduce data redundancy; highlights and helps to enforce an organization's business rules; is unambiguous; is adaptable; is simple and concise, often referred to as elegant; communicates effectively; and helps ensure that the database will integrate well with the organization's other databases. A good data model is complete, highlights and helps to enforce an organization's business rules.

7) The correct answer choice is "C".

8) The correct answer choice is "D".

9) True.

Document and Content Management

Educational Objectives

Upon completion of this assignment, you should be able to:

1. Define and describe document and content management.
2. Outline the document management life cycle.
3. Describe the activities involved in document management and content management.
4. Describe the methods used to index and retrieve content.
5. Describe the risks associated with document and content management and how they can be mitigated.
6. Describe the issues related to document and content retention and destruction.
7. Describe audit protocols in document and content management.
8. List the guiding principles of content and document management.
9. Define structured and unstructured data. Provide examples of each.
10. Define multi-structured data. Provide an example.
11. Define data mining and text mining.
12. Describe the importance of unstructured data to organizations.
13. Outline the challenges involved in managing unstructured data.
14. Describe the challenges of integrating structured and unstructured data.

For each assignment, define or describe each of the Key Terms and Concepts and answer each of the Review and Discussion Questions.

Key Terms and Concepts

Document management

Content management

Content architecture

Full text indexing

Field text indexing

Structured data

Unstructured data

Textual unstructured data

Nontextual unstructured data

Highly structured data

Complex structured data

Multi-structured data

Data mining

Knowledge discovery from data (KDD)

Text mining

Text analytics

Review Questions

1) Define and describe document and content management.

2) Outline the document management life cycle.

3) Describe the activities involved in document management and content management.

4) Which one of the following statement is NOT true when describing the issues related to document and content retention and destruction?

   A. Retention requirements for certain types of documents are established by regulatory bodies. Organizations need to be aware of all applicable records-retention legislation and regulations, and ensure that they are in compliance.

   B. All personally identifiable information (PII) and personal health information (PHI), also referred to as Individually Identifiable Health Information, are subject to 15 years retention requirement.

   C. Documents that are not subject to regulatory retention requirements and that are no longer of value to an organization should be disposed of in an appropriate manner.

   D. None of the above.

5) Describe audit protocols in document and content management.

6) List the guiding principles of content and document management.

7) Define structured and unstructured data. Provide examples of each.

8) Define multi-structured data. Provide an example.

9) Describe the importance of unstructured data to organizations.

10) Outline the challenges involved in managing unstructured data.

11) Describe the challenges of integrating structured and unstructured data.

12) Which of the following does document management focus on?

A. The document as a whole.

B. The data elements within the document.

C. The portions of the document which are textual.

D. The unstructured content of the document.

13) Name some of the goals of document and content management.

14) Document management lifecycle involves which of the following?

A. Auditing the effectiveness of an organization's policies, procedures, and systems.

B. Implementing document control and retention policies.

C. Allowing access in accordance with policies, standards, and regulations.

D. Archiving and appropriately destroying documents.

15) What type of structured data is a photograph with a time stamp?

A. Structured.

B. Highly structured.

C. Complex structured.

D. Multi-structured.

16) Which type of structured data is more intricately structured than traditional tabular data?

A. Unstructured.

B. Structured.

C. Highly structured.

D. Multi-structured.

17) What process involves: planning, establishing responsibilities; selecting samples and reporting results?

A. Quality data management.

B. Content quality management.

C. Audit protocols.

D. Record retention.

18) A controlled vocabulary is simply a set of agreed upon terms that are clearly defined, consistently used, and formally managed with rules about how terms are added, modified, or deleted is part of which indexing approach?

    A. Word text indexing.

    B. Formula text indexing.

    C. Full text indexing.

    D. Field text indexing.

19) True or false: Document management focuses on the document as a whole rather than on the content elements it contains.

Discussion Questions

NOTE: The below questions are intended to continue to challenge you to test your knowledge of the required reading by applying what you have studied to real-life situations.

No suggested answers are provided at the end of the assignment for these types of open discussion questions. Answers may vary by student and will depend on their organization's culture, resources, and processes!

1) Unstructured data are important because they can offer insights far beyond those that can be gleaned from structured data alone. For example, consider an insurer's customer service call center. If calls are recorded and subsequently transcribed and analyzed, they could reveal a wealth of information about customers' attitudes, needs, and preferences. That information could enhance relationships with individual customers, and lead to innovations in products and services that would give the insurer a competitive advantage. Give at least four examples of how unstructured data benefits your organization.

2) Name some of the multi-structured data available in your organization.

3) Give at least four examples of the risks to data in a database.

Answers to Assignment 10 Questions

NOTE: These answers are provided to give students a basic understanding of acceptable types of responses. They are often not the only valid answers and are not intended to provide an exhaustive response to the questions.

Key Terms and Concepts

Document management: Sometimes referred to as records management, is a collection of systems, either manual or electronic, used to maintain, classify, organize, and retrieve paper or electronic documents.

Content management: The organizing, categorizing, and structuring of information resources so that they can be stored, published, and reused in multiple ways.

Content architecture: A logical way of organizing content so that the information it contains can be readily discovered, accessed, used and reused.

Full text indexing: The technique of indexing to include every word on every page. Full text indexing supports flexibility in search terminology and allows for the discovery of documents. Allows for discovery of documents about which the searcher is unaware.

Field text indexing: An indexing technique based on a set of agreed upon terms that are clearly defined, consistently used, and formally managed with rules about how terms are added, modified, or deleted. It includes a limited selection of metadata in the index. Efficiently retrieves a specific document but cannot discover a document about which the searcher is unaware.

Structured data: Data that are organized in a pre-defined manner.

Unstructured data: Data that cannot be stored in, or accessed from, traditional databases. They may have few formal requirements, or do not have a patterned organization.

Textual unstructured data: Data that is textual but cannot be stored in, or accessed from, traditional databases. Examples are word processing documents, emails, and text messages.

Nontextual unstructured data: Data that are graphical and cannot be stored in, or accessed from, traditional databases. Examples include such things as photographs, diagrams, X-rays, and audio or video recordings.

Highly structured data: Data that are more intricately structured than traditional tabular data, but are not as intricately structured as complex structured data.

Complex structured data: Any data that are composed of two or more intricate, complicated, and interrelated parts that cannot be easily interpreted by structured query languages and tools.

Multi-structured data: Data that are made up of two or more varieties of structured data.

Data mining: The process of sifting through large amounts of data using pattern recognition and other knowledge discovery statistical techniques to identify previously undiscovered and potentially meaningful data content, relationships, and trends.

Knowledge discovery from data (KDD): The set of processes such as data mining, text mining, and text analytics for deriving business value from data.

Text mining: A type of data mining that focuses on the automated discovery of knowledge from large amounts of textual records, such as documents, emails, correspondence, or social media.

Text analytics: Text mining used to solve business problems.

Review Questions

1) Document and content management is defined as the control over capture, storage, access and use of data and information stored outside structured databases. These data and information may be in a variety of forms including paper documents, electronic word processing documents, emails, scanned copies of paper documents, spreadsheets, photographs, audio and video recordings, and intranet content.

2) Document management lifecycle, which involves all of an organization's documents and includes a number of steps:

   - Identification of existing and newly created documents/records.
   - Creation, approval, and enforcement of documents/records policies, including retention policies.
   - Classification of documents/records.
   - Short and long term storage of physical and electronic documents/records.
   - Allowing access and circulation of documents/records in accordance with policies, security and control standards, and legal requirements.
   - Archiving and destroying documents/records according to organizational needs, statutes, and regulations.

3) Document management involves a number of activities: Planning; Implementing document management systems; Backing up and recovering documents; Retaining and disposing of documents, and; Auditing.

   Activities essential to effective content management are: Defining content architecture; Developing effective metadata; Providing content access, and; Governing for quality.

4) The correct answer choice is "B".

5) Periodic auditing is important to ensure the effectiveness and compliance of an organization's document and content management policies, procedures, and systems.

   An audit typically involves the following steps: Planning; Establishing responsibilities; Selecting samples; Performing the audit, and; Reporting results.

6) There are three guiding principles in content and document management:

   - Everyone in an organization has a role to play in protecting its future. Everyone must create, use, retrieve, and dispose of records in accordance with the established policies and procedures.
   - Experts in the handling of records and content should be fully engaged in policy and planning. Regulatory and best practices can vary significantly based on industry sector and legal jurisdiction.
   - Even if records management professionals are not available to the organization, everyone can be trained and have an understanding of the issues. Once trained, business stewards, and others can collaborate on an effective approach to records management.

7) Structured data are data that are organized in a pre-defined manner. Structured data are often generated by transactions and each type of structured data has a consistent format. For example, the data contained in automobile insurance applications can be captured and stored in various tables in an insurer's relational database. In this case, the structured data are erred to as "tabular data".

   Unstructured data are data that are not structured, have few formal requirements, or do not have a patterned organization. Unstructured data cannot easily be converted to a tabular form, and they cannot be stored in, or accessed from, traditional databases. Unstructured data can be classified as textual or nontextual. Unstructured data can be classified as textual or nontextual. Examples of textual unstructured data include word processing documents, emails, and text messages. Nontextual unstructured data include such things as photographs, diagrams, X-rays, and audio or video recordings.

8) Multi-structured data are data that are made up of two or more varieties of structured data. For example, a photograph would be categorized as complex structured data. However, that photograph may have an associated GPS location, date stamp, or time stamp, all of which are structured data. Some data management professionals consider multi-structured data to be a subset of complex structured data; others feel that the term "multi-structured data" more clearly describes this particular type of data.

9) It has been estimated that as much as 80 percent of business data and information are unstructured. Unstructured data are important because they can offer insights far beyond those that can be gleaned from structured data alone. If calls are recorded and subsequently transcribed and analyzed, they could reveal a wealth of information about customers' attitudes, needs, and preferences. That information could enhance relationships with individual customers, and lead to innovations in products and services that would give the insurer a competitive advantage.

10) Organizations are collecting and creating more and more unstructured data in a variety of formats, and the pace of that growth is accelerating. This ever increasing volume and variety can be a challenge to manage. As well, unstructured data are typically distributed throughout an organization and it can be difficult to determine what data an organization actually has. Inefficiencies result when the same task, for example preparing a slide presentation or report, is performed multiple times because there is no effective way of determining that the presentation or report already exists, locating it, and accessing it. In addition, it can be challenging to decide what unstructured data an organization needs to capture, analyze and keep, without exacerbating the challenges inherent in unstructured data.

    In order to be able to analyze textual unstructured data, the data need to be transformed in a variety of ways. One challenge involves determining which data are of importance and value to an organization; preparing unstructured textual data for analysis involves differences in vocabulary and expression. Different individuals express the same concept or idea differently.

    A further challenge relates to metadata. Traditionally, metadata have been associated with structured data. However, if textual unstructured data are to be included in data warehouses and used in analytics, high-quality metadata are essential.

11) There are technical challenges involved in integrating unstructured data with other enterprise systems. Organizations need enhanced storage and processing capabilities to deal with the huge additional volume of unstructured data. The tools available may not meet organizations' needs or may be perceived as too complex or costly. Finally, the business need for unstructured data may not be well understood or defined.

12) The correct answer choice is "A".

13) Document and content management fulfill the following goals: Safeguard; Retrieval and use Compliance; Business continuity; and Cost control.

14) The correct answer choice is "A".

15) The correct answer choice is "D".

16) The correct answer choice is "C".

17) The correct answer choice is "C".

18) The correct answer choice is "D".

19) True.

Business Analytics and Predictive Modeling Overview

Educational Objectives

Upon completion of this assignment, you should be able to:

1. Describe business performance management (BPM).
2. Describe how data warehousing supports BPM.
3. Describe how to process data for business intelligence.
4. Define and contrast the concepts of strategic, tactical, and operational business intelligence.
5. Describe how the vocabulary of data warehousing and business intelligence is changing.
6. Define analytics.
7. Briefly describe the three disciplines of analytics.
8. Define business analytics.
9. Define predictive modeling.
10. List the five steps in building a predictive model.
11. Explain how business intelligence (BI) and predictive modeling impact the development of databases.

For each assignment, define or describe each of the Key Terms and Concepts and answer each of the Review and Discussion Questions.

Key Terms and Concepts

Business performance management (BPM)

Key performance indicator (KPI)

Dashboard

Extract-transform-load (ETL)

Source-to-target mapping

Full extraction

Incremental extraction

Strategic BI

Tactical BI

Operational BI

Analytics

Predictive analytics

Prescriptive analytics

Predictive modeling

Latency

Online analytical processing (OLAP)

Dimension

Review Questions

1) How does data warehousing supports business performance management BPM?

2) Describe how to process data for business intelligence.

3) Define and contrast the concepts of strategic, tactical, and operational business intelligence.

4) Describe how the vocabulary of data warehousing and business intelligence is changing.

5) Briefly describe the three disciplines of analytics.

6) Define business analytics.

7) List the five steps in building a predictive model.

8) Explain how business intelligence (BI) and predictive modeling impact the development of databases.

9) Which one of the following statements is NOT True?

   A. Source-to-target mapping is an integral component of data warehouse development.

   B. Data warehousing provides access to the information that facilitates business performance management.

   C. Typically, the data in a data warehouse or data mart originate from a variety of internal and external sources and systems, and they exist in a variety of sometimes incompatible formats.

   D. Tactical planning facilitates completion of the activities identified in operational planning.

10) True or false, full extraction is more complex to perform than incremental extraction.

11) True or false, traditional data warehouses were typically updated on a weekly.

Discussion Questions

NOTE: The below questions are intended to continue to challenge you to test your knowledge of the required reading by applying what you have studied to real-life situations.

No suggested answers are provided at the end of the assignment for these types of open discussion questions. Answers may vary by student and will depend on their organization's culture, resources, and processes!

1) Name a few key performance indicators that are used at your organization.

2) Give some examples of how predictive modeling may be used at your organization.

3) Explain why 'source-to-target' mapping is better described as 'target-from-source'.

Answers to Assignment 11 Questions

NOTE: These answers are provided to give students a basic understanding of acceptable types of responses. They are often not the only valid answers and are not intended to provide an exhaustive response to the questions.

Key Terms and Concepts

Business performance management (BPM): A set of methodologies and tools that help organizations optimize their performance and make better use of their financial, human, and data resources.

Key performance indicator (KPI): A metric used to measure an organization's effectiveness.

Dashboard: A business intelligence application that consolidates, aggregates, and graphically presents performance measurements compared to goals, arranged so that information can be monitored at a glance.

Extract-transform-load (ETL): The process performed to populate a data warehouse with disparate data from a variety of sources and to ensure that the data in the warehouse are of high quality.

Source-to-target mapping: The documentation activity that defines data type details and transformation rules for all required entities and data elements, and from each individual source to each individual target.

Full extraction: One of two ETL data extraction process methods in which all of the required data are copied from the data source.

Incremental extraction: One of two ETL data extraction process methods in which only those data that have changed since the last extraction are copied.

Strategic BI: An approach of business planning that forms part of a formal business performance management (BPM) program to allow executives and senior managers to plan and monitor key performance indicators.

Tactical BI: An approach of business planning focuses on the activities identified and selected during tactical planning and monitoring performance indicators.

Operational BI: An approach of business planning which allows an organization to manage and optimize its business operations or allocate resources.

Analytics: The data, tools, and applications that support corporate strategic plans and business performance; they provide the ability to gather, store, access, and analyze corporate data for decision making.

Predictive analytics: Focuses on determining what is likely to happen in the future based on historical trends and other data.

Prescriptive analytics: Helps managers choose the best course of action when a decision needs to be made.

Predictive modeling: The process of analyzing data to create a statistical model of future behavior.

Latency: The time delay for data to be updated in a system.

Online analytical processing (OLAP): A method for summarizing or viewing data to allow managers to query the data warehouse and data marts in interactive sessions and to perform multi-dimensional analysis.

Dimension: Categories for summarizing or viewing data (e.g. sales by region, by quarter, and product) are referred to as a dimension.

Review Questions

1) Owing to the two elements of data warehousing, the internal and external software and the resulting database, it can support BPM by enhancing an organization's ability to access and analyze data. Businesses can use historical and current data for predictive analytics.

2) Data can be processed through an integrative and iterative process, ongoing processes such as ETL for strategic, tactical, and operational business intelligence.

3) Strategic, tactical, and operational are the various approaches to business intelligence (BI) to achieve an organization's objectives.

   Strategic BI is the approach used by executives and senior managers with an aim to monitor key performance indicators (KPI). Whereas tactical BI is used by managers and analysts to measure KPI periodically, while operational BI is used by managers and supervisors to measure daily or real-time information about transactions or processes.

4) The vocabulary and terminology used in data warehousing and business intelligence has changed with time by creation of new terminology and repurposing of the old for marketing of the various hardware and software solutions.

5) The three disciplines of analytics are descriptive, predictive, and prescriptive. Descriptive analytics is used for depiction of a past or current state; predictive analytics are useful for prediction of the future based on historical trend, whereas prescriptive analytics is chosen by managers for decision-making.

6) Business analytics is a set of solution including data mining, predictive analytics, and applied statistics used for development of models and simulation to assist industry business processes.

7) Retrieve and organize the data; Understand the data; Split the data and build a model; Evaluate the model's performance, and; Iterate and choose a model.

8) Databases designed for use in data warehouses and data marts focus on facilitating analysis. Managers and analysts use these databases to gain an understanding of the business and predictive modeling. Each analytic query can involve many records, in some cases millions, and the amount of data under analysis is generally quite large. The underlying data must support the analytics and predictive needs; hence as time progresses, databases are developed to support the demands of BI and predictive modeling.

9) The correct answer choice is "D".

10) False. Incremental extraction is more complex to perform than full extraction.

11) False. Traditional data warehouses were typically updated daily, in an overnight batch process.

Data Management Trends, Technologies, and Frameworks

Educational Objectives

Upon completion of this assignment, you should be able to:

1. Describe how tools facilitate the data management functions.
2. List general types of tools that would be of use to a data manager.
3. Describe the issues to consider when determining whether to build or purchase tools.
4. Describe the data manager's role in building or purchasing tools.
5. Describe the IDMA approach to evaluating tools.
6. Define XML.
7. Describe the impact of XML.
8. Describe how frameworks assist data managers.
9. Describe how a framework is useful in change management.
10. Describe some common frameworks.
11. Discuss enterprise data strategy and its objectives.

For each assignment, define or describe each of the Key Terms and Concepts and answer each of the Review and Discussion Questions.

Key Terms and Concepts

Extensible markup language (XML)

Enterprise architecture

Ontology

Enterprise data strategy

Review Questions

1) Describe how tools facilitate the data management functions?

2) Describe the issues to consider when determining whether to build or purchase tools.

3) Describe the data manager's role in building or purchasing tools.

4) Describe the IDMA approach to evaluating tools.

5) Describe the impact of XML.

6) Describe how frameworks assist data managers.

7) Describe how a framework is useful in change management.

8) Describe some common frameworks.

9) Which of the following are NOT data management tools?

   A. Data modeling tools.

   B. Business intelligence tools.

   C. Document management tools.

   D. Enterprise data strategy tools.

10) Which one of the following is NOT a principle consideration in determining whether to buy or build a metadata repository?

    A. Cost.

    B. Culture.

    C. Classification.

    D. Capabilities.

11) An enterprise data strategy focuses on achieving a number of objectives. Which one the following is not one of those objectives?

    A. Supporting flexibility and agility in a rapidly changing environment.

    B. Minimizing usage of external data sources.

    C. Consolidating data architecture to optimize information delivery.

    D. Increasing integration and alignment among the functional areas.

12) Which one of the following statements is NOT true?

    A. Ontology is a semantic data model defining structure and meaning typically used to model non-tabular data.

    B. An enterprise data strategy is a plan for improving the way an enterprise leverages its data, allowing the company to turn data into information and knowledge which, in turn, produce measurable improvements in business performance.

    C. An organization's culture can have a significant impact on the decision to buy or build a system.

    D. None of the above.

13) The Open Group Architecture Framework (TOGAF) is designed as a practical approach to developing an enterprise architecture and it includes three elements. Which of the following is not an element of TOGAF?

    A. An Architecture Development Method (ADM).

    B. A Scope Contexts.

    C. An Enterprise Continuum.

    D. A Resource Base.

14) True or false, it should be the IT side of the organization that drives its enterprise data strategy, rather than the business side?

15) True or false, the Architecture Development Method (ADM) explains how to design an enterprise architecture that best meets an organization's needs?

Discussion Questions

NOTE: The below questions are intended to continue to challenge you to test your knowledge of the required reading by applying what you have studied to real-life situations.

No suggested answers are provided at the end of the assignment for these types of open discussion questions. Answers may vary by student and will depend on their organization's culture, resources, and processes!

1) Give some benefits of XML and examples of how XML is used or can be used in your organization.

2) Why is it important to identify any architectural requirements while evaluating tools?

3) Explain why an increasingly changing environment is challenging to data managers with respect to techniques, technologies, and solutions.

Answers to Assignment 12 Questions

NOTE: These answers are provided to give students a basic understanding of acceptable types of responses. They are often not the only valid answers and are not intended to provide an exhaustive response to the questions.

Key Terms and Concepts

Extensible markup language (XML): A tag-based markup language defined by W3C (World Wide Web Consortium Organization) with a tag set that can be added to enable XML documents to be self-describing structures.

Enterprise architecture: An integrated collection of models and design approaches used to align information, processes, projects, and technology with the goals of the enterprise.

Ontology: A semantic data model defining structure and meaning typically used to model non-tabular data.

Enterprise data strategy: A plan for improving the way an enterprise leverages its data, allowing the company to turn data into information and knowledge which, in turn, produce measurable improvements in business performance.

Review Questions

1) Tools facilitate data management in a variety of ways, depending on the data management function being performed. Issues management tools can help in data governance activities, while graphic illustration tools help data architecture management, data modeling functions. The data operations management function relies on robust database management systems (DBMS) and database administration tools to manage the lifecycle of the organization's structured data. Data security management use identity authentication tools and data warehousing and business intelligence management use extract, transform and load tools, data discovery and visualization tools, and statistical analysis tools.

2) When deciding about building or purchasing tools, some issues to consider are the resulting tool's capabilities, cost, customization, and culture for optimal results.

3) A data manager may decide to buy or build tools based on their own and organizational skills, company structure and culture.

4) In the process of buying or building tools, a data manager may perform some or all of the following:

   - Plan,
   - Budget,
   - Recruit,
   - Consult IT staff,
   - Evaluate products and vendors,
   - Determine criteria and method of evaluation, and
   - Analyze and recommend the results.

5) IDMA approach in evaluating tools is to discern different evaluation criteria for different sources. The technical environment, culture, and methodologies of the organization and whether the tool is being

purchased or built must be conducive to documentation and ongoing support for all users. Data management professionals typically consider the extent, ease and cost for the tool to meet the identified business need; business rules, support the volume demands, and structure or maturity.

XML facilitates the automated sharing of data among different applications and databases. XML can be used to link legacy systems and newer systems, including intranets and the Web. XML is simply a language used to describe data so that it can be understood and manipulated by other tools. XML benefits businesses in standardization, manageability, longevity, B2B and B2C communication, extensibility, human and machine interfaces, and internationalization.

6) Frameworks assist data managers by providing an approach to conceptualizing complex situations or problems; and a structured way in which to manage complex situations or resolve problems.

7) Frameworks are essential in that they help an organization take a structured, cohesive, and manageable approach to designing and deploying an enterprise architecture in managing cost, time and innovation issues.

8) Some common frameworks may be used individually or in combination based on the different approaches. For example, the ACORD Framework was developed in response to a recognized need for enterprise architecture within the insurance industry, the Zachman framework supports a structured way of thinking about enterprise and its architecture, and TOGAF comprises a set of tools and methodologies that can be used to develop a range of IT architectures including an enterprise architecture.

9) The correct answer choice is “D”.

10) The correct answer choice is “C”.

11) The correct answer choice is “B”.

12) The correct answer choice is “D”.

13) The correct answer choice is “B”.

14) False. It should be the business side of the organization that drives its enterprise data strategy, rather than the IT side.

15) True.

What We Learned From IDMA 201

Educational Objective

The objective of this final assignment is to apply the knowledge learned from the IDMA 201 course to business environments **through case studies** that focus on the following:

- Tools and methodologies used to derive how an efficient and effective data management culture is established;
- Issues challenging data management to maintain competitive advantage; and,
- Best practices in data management in a continually changing environment.

Case Studies

NOTE: The case studies provided in this assignment are intended to challenge you to test your knowledge by applying what you have learned throughout the entire course to real-life situations.

Answers are provided at the end of the assignment to give students a basic understanding of acceptable types of responses. They are often not the only valid answers and are not intended to provide an exhaustive response to the questions.

Case Study #1

The technology environment has changed dramatically over the past several years, and your company has a strong interest in leveraging a service-oriented architecture (SOA) for competitive advantage. Your chief technology officer (CTO) has made a strong case for taking your company's core applications to the next generation architecture to build on your technology leadership within the insurance industry. There is a desire to develop products that are highly interoperable, location-transparent, and capable of integrating with other industry applications and data sources.

As the chief data officer (CDO), you are required to provide your expert opinion and signoff on these changes. You have worked diligently over the past two years to establish data-maintenance and governance processes and procedures, to maintain accurate master data. You are concerned that these proposed changes will adversely impact the business processes and controls that you have worked so hard at putting into place.

Questions:

1) Master data management (MDM) is the process of defining how master data will be created, maintained, and integrated for general use. What is needed to maintain an MDM environment to promote interoperability?

2) What is a golden record?

Case Study #2

Executives at an insurance company who have a strong desire to develop an effective data management culture within their organization hire you as a consultant. The executive team has shared with you that they are having trouble motivating their middle managers and front-line supervisors to take action to improve the quality of the organization's data assets. The management team feels that they are constantly under pressure to work leaner and smarter. Data quality is not on the top of their priority list.

A number of consultants before you have recommended changes to technology. The company has moved forward with implementing these changes. However, just last month, the company came under scrutiny by a number of state regulators for furnishing information that was incomplete and inconsistent with past information. The executive team fears that they have made poor choices and wrong investments, and there is little hope to turn around this situation.

Questions:

1) What would be your top recommendation to the executive team on how to successfully cultivate an effective enterprise data management culture?

2) What major components should be included in an enterprise data strategy in order to be successful?

3) What should be your response to the executive team that "data quality is not on the top of their priority list"? (i.e., Why you must recommend that the organization invest in data quality tools and projects.)

Case Study #3

As a data manager, you are faced with a number of challenges, since we operate in an environment that is continuously changing. Professional data managers should ensure that they keep current. New techniques, technologies, and solutions, designed to meet businesses' evolving operational, analytic, and data management requirements, emerge regularly.

Questions:

1) Tools can be purchased from a vendor or developed in-house. What are the principle considerations that you should take into account when determining whether to buy a tool from a vendor or build it in-house?

2) When evaluating a tool, data management professionals typically consider a variety of factors. List a few of these factors.

3) Staying up to date in an industry that is constantly shifting is not easy, but being aware of changes as they are happening can keep you ahead of the curve. List some of the ways, channels, and tools that data managers are utilizing to help them stay current on industry trends.

Answers to Assignment 13 Questions

NOTE: These answers are provided to give students a basic understanding of acceptable types of responses. They are often not the only valid answers and are not intended to provide an exhaustive response to the questions.

Case Studies

Case Study #1

1) In order to maintain an MDM environment and promote interoperability, appropriate data governance must be implemented and ongoing master data quality must be maintained. Also, determining how master data should be managed and how it should be used is essential.
2) The golden record encompasses the most accurate and complete data in every system of record within a particular organization.

Case Study #2

1) Enterprise data management, often referred to as enterprise information management (EIM), is essentially "data management performed with an enterprise-wide mandate". Major changes to culture should emanate from the executive level, and an executive champion should be appointed to lead this effort.
2) Successful implementation of an EIM strategy requires careful planning, strong leadership, a considerable investment, and significant technical expertise. It may also require the organization to restructure itself, its business processes, and its internal and external relationships.

EIM initiatives are more likely to succeed with the following components in place:

- An EIM champion at the senior level within the organization.
- Clearly defined data governance and stewardship roles, responsibilities, processes, and policies to ensure that governance can be sustained over the long term.
- Establishing meaningful metrics to measure the impact of implementing EIM.
- Metadata management.
- A sound data model for an enterprise-wide architecture.

3) You must recommend that the organization invest in data quality tools and projects because:

- Information is essential to all of an organization's activities. Information is derived from data, therefore the quality of those data is critical.
- Controlling data is an important aspect of managing. Data quality controls are needed to ensure that an organization meets its goals.
- Errors can occur in virtually any process where data is acquired, stored, selected, retrieved, transformed, manipulated and presented. Data quality measures are crucial in minimizing, if not eliminating minimizing, data errors.
- Data quality helps set standards that improve the materials, products and processes that a company provides.

Case Study #3

1) Principle considerations that you should be taken into account when determining whether to buy a tool from a vendor or build it in house are:

- Capabilities – It is important to assess the capabilities of the organization's data managers and IT professionals. Do they have the expertise required to design, build, and maintain a tool in-house?
- Cost (both financial cost and opportunity cost) – A cost-benefit analysis can often help determine whether buying or building would be the better approach for a particular organization or situation.
- Customization – A vendor's product may not meet all of an organization's needs.
- Culture – Some organizations simply have a preference for purchasing solutions while others prefer to develop them internally.

2) When evaluating a tool, data management professionals typically consider a variety of factors including such things as the following:

- The extent to which the tool meets the identified business need and whether it can be customized.
- How easy and intuitive the tool is to use, particularly by non-technical staff.
- The total cost of ownership, including acquisition costs, licensing fees, support, and maintenance.
- The tool's architecture and how it will integrate with the organization's other systems.
- Whether the tool includes a business rules engine that allows non-programmers to add or change business rules.
- Whether the tool can support the expected volume of data and number of concurrent users, and the extent to which it can scale up as needed.
- The types of data the tool can handle, for example highly structured or complex structured data.
- The maturity of the technology and any plans the vendor has for development or enhancement of the tool.
- The amount of training and technical support that the vendor is able to provide
- The extent to which the vendor is well-established and financially stable.

3) Here are a few recommendations on how to keep up with industry trends:

- Subscribe to trade journals.
- Keep up with consumer magazines.
- Join an industry association.
- Get out to conferences or local events, and sign up for trainings.
- Scan and engage in forums and discussion boards.
- Scour website and blogs.
- Listen to/watch podcasts and webinars.
- Talk to your customer.
- Observe your competitors.